W9-BDA-946

CULTURES OF THE WORLD®

CANADA

Guek-Cheng Pang

BENCHMARK **B**OOKS

MARSHALL CAVENDISH
NEW YORK

Humber College Library

PICTURE CREDITS
Cover: © Art Directors/Norman Price
AFP/CORBIS: 39 • APA: 10, 12, 13, 66, 86, 102 • Archive Photos: 28 • Art Directors & TRIP: 114
• Niall Benvie/CORBIS: 9 • British High Commission, Singapore: 36 • Canada-ASEAN Centre/Expo '86:
51 • Canada-ASEAN Centre/Isolde Ohlbaum: 100 • Canada-ASEAN Centre/ISTC: 3, 8, 15, 23, 82, 92,
111, 118, 119, 124, 128 • Canada-ASEAN Centre/MEDIT: 80 • Canada-ASEAN Centre/Province of British
Columbia: 110 • Canada-ASEAN Centre/Alberta Tourism: 4, 17 • Dave G. Houser/Houserstock: 122 • Eye
Ubiquitous/Laurence Fordyce: 44 • Rankin Harvey: 6 • Hulton-Deutsch: 25, 30, 37, 40, 105 • Hutchison
Library: 26, 57, 76, 115 • Image Bank: 11, 14, 18, 27, 31, 38, 43, 45, 46, 47, 48, 49, 63, 64, 88, 98, 108, 109,
116, 117, 120, 125, 126 • Jan Butchofsky-Houser/Houserstock: 34, 72 • Mathieu Lamarre: 55 • Life File
Photo Library: 16, 50 • Guek-Cheng Pang: 130, 131 • Photobank International: 5, 20, 56, 61 • Pietro
Scozzari: 96 • David Simson: 32, 33, 42, 65, 67, 68, 69, 70, 74, 77, 78, 81, 83, 91, 93, 94, 95, 99, 103,
104, 112, 113, 123 • Travel Ink: 59, 106 • Nik Wheeler: 84, 90 • Alison Wright: 1, 51, 54, 62, 129

ACKNOWLEDGMENTS
Thanks to Betsy Arntzen, Education Outreach Coordinator for the Canadian-American Center at
the University of Maine, for her expert reading of this manuscript. Thanks also to Susan Newton
for preparing the bannock and nanaimo bar for the recipe photography.

PRECEDING PAGE
Members of a dragon-boat club paddle away in Kelowna, British Columbia. Every year, the province
hosts North America's biggest dragon-boat event, the Alcan Dragon Boat Festival, in Vancouver.

Marshall Cavendish Benchmark
99 White Plains Road
Tarrytown, NY 10591
Website: www.marshallcavendish.us

© Times Media Private Limited 1996, 1994
© Marshall Cavendish International (Asia) Private Limited 2004
All rights reserved. First edition 1994. Second edition 2004.

Originated and designed by Times Books International
An imprint of Marshall Cavendish International (Asia) Private Limited
A member of Times Publishing Limited

Library of Congress Cataloging-in-Publication Data
Pang, Guek-Cheng, 1950-
Canada / by Guek-Cheng Pang. — 2nd ed.
   p. cm. — (Cultures of the world)
Includes bibliographical references (p.) and index.
   ISBN 0-7614-1788-5
1. Canada—Juvenile literature. I. Title. II. Series: Cultures of the world (2nd ed.).
F1008.2.C44 2004
971—dc22   2004008584

Printed in China

7 6 5 4 3 2

CONTENTS

Farmers have their lunch in Saskatchewan, one of the main grain-growing regions of Canada.

Deer hunters stalk their quarry near Whitecourt in Alberta.

INTRODUCTION

SINCE THE 1990S Canada has come into its own. For seven consecutive years, the United Nations Human Development Program (UNHDP) has rated Canada the most desirable place on earth to live. Canadians have a young, bright, and forward-looking outlook. They have a somewhat conservative and quiet tone, which they may have inherited from the early British settlers who chose to remain aligned with the British Crown and not participate in the American revolution.

Canadians also treasure the uniqueness of their French heritage. Non-indigenous Canadians have also developed a greater understanding and appreciation of the rich tradition that the first peoples of the land have bequeathed to the country. Whether of indigenous, European, Asian, or other ethnic origin, Canada's people are a diverse lot who have come together not in a melting pot that blends their separate flavors but in a mosaic with many distinctly different colors and textures.

GEOGRAPHY

CANADA IS THE SECOND-LARGEST country in the world. Its land area totals more than 3.8 million square miles (9.8 million square km). Only Russia is bigger than Canada. Despite its size, Canada is one of the most sparsely populated countries in the world.

Politically, Canada is divided into 10 provinces and three territories. Creations of the Constitution Act, the provinces are self-governing. The territories, with their smaller populations, were established by federal law and are controlled by the federal government.

Opposite: **Steep cliffs and gushing waterfalls flank a trail winding through Johnston Canyon in Banff National Park, Alberta.**

SIX REGIONS

Geographically, Canada has six distinct regions. The Appalachian region covers the provinces of Newfoundland and Labrador, Prince Edward Island, Nova Scotia, New Brunswick, and the southeastern extremity of Quebec. The region is characterized by forested hills and a rugged and indented coastline washed by the Atlantic Ocean.

The Great Lakes-Saint Lawrence lowlands, part of the provinces of Ontario and Quebec, is home to more than half of Canada's population and has a rich agricultural and commercial life. North of the lowlands, occupying about half the mainland, is the Canadian Shield, a glacially eroded region of rivers, lakes, and forests that is practically uninhabitable. The region's population is concentrated along the southern border.

The interior plains or prairies are the largest area of nearly flat land in Canada. The region is bounded on the west by the Rocky Mountains and on the east by the Canadian Shield. The Western Cordillera is a region of mountains, plateaus, and valleys that extends from the Rocky Mountains to the Coast Mountains flanking the Pacific Ocean, and north through the Yukon Territory into Alaska. The sixth region is the North, a resource-rich, harsh, and essentially treeless environment with an arctic climate.

PROVINCE BY PROVINCE

NEWFOUNDLAND AND LABRADOR This is the most easterly of the provinces. The larger, mainland part of the province is Labrador, a land of rocks, swamps, and lakes. Its rugged coastline has promontories that rise directly from the sea. People here live physically isolated lives, and often boats are their only means of transportation.

Newfoundland is a mountainous island with a rocky, rugged coast. There are few big cities in this part of the province, and life is centered around small fishing villages. The land is rich in minerals, and the development of the island's natural resources is an important part of the province's economy. Iron ore and recently discovered offshore oil and gas deposits are the greatest sources of the region's wealth. Pulp and paper and food processing are the main manufacturing industries, while tourism is fast becoming another important industry.

The capital of Newfoundland, St. John's, is one of the oldest cities in North America and was England's first overseas colony.

PRINCE EDWARD ISLAND Prince Edward Island, or PEI, is the country's smallest but most densely populated province. The province's rich, red soil supports a large farming community that produces potatoes as its main crop. Fishing, especially for lobsters, is another important industry in PEI. The capital, Charlottetown, is known as the Cradle of Confederation because it was

St. John's in Newfoundland was the first place in Canada to be colonized by British settlers.

FISHING CRISIS

Until 1992 cod fishing was the main industry in most of Atlantic Canada. However, government mismanagement and domestic and foreign overfishing, among other developments, led to the depletion of fish stocks to such an extent that the government had to impose a moratorium on cod fishing. This caused the industry to collapse.

Since then, the Canadian government has spent billions of dollars on conservation plans to replenish the Atlantic cod population and on job retraining programs to equip unemployed fishermen with the skills that they need to make their transition out of fishing and into other industries.

However, despite the government's actions, the cod population remains unstable, and only time will tell if cod fishing will ever regain its former position of importance in the Canadian economy.

the site of the historic meeting in 1864 that eventually led to the unification of Canada in 1867.

NOVA SCOTIA Like its neighboring provinces, Nova Scotia has a rugged coastline punctuated by numerous bays and inlets—ideal sites for fishing villages.

Mining forms a major part of the Nova Scotian economy, along with tourism and manufacturing. Livestock raising and fruit farming are also important economic activities. Forests occupy about 71 percent of Nova Scotia. The provincial government owns only about one quarter of this woodland, and most of it is used for public parks and reserves. Because of the abundance of forest reserves, hunting—especially for deer and moose—is a favorite outdoor sport for tourists and Nova Scotians alike.

Halifax, the provincial capital and one of the country's main ports, has one of the world's best natural harbors and is the Atlantic headquarters of Canada's navy.

If the 31.6 million people who live in Canada were to be evenly spread out, there would be roughly 8.3 people per square mile (3.2 people per square km).

NEW BRUNSWICK Nearly rectangular in shape and with an extensive coastline, New Brunswick is an undulating, heavily forested land. New Brunswick shares the Bay of Fundy with Nova Scotia.

The Saint John River Valley is a fertile oasis that supports farming in New Brunswick. Potatoes, vegetables, cattle, poultry, and pork are the province's major produce. Forest products and food processing are the main manufacturing industries. Zinc, potash, and lead are important minerals. The main catch of the province's fisheries is lobster and crab.

Fredericton is the capital of New Brunswick, and Saint John is its main port and industrial center.

Horseshoe Falls in Ontario is part of the world-famous Niagara Falls, which Canada shares with the United States.

QUEBEC This is the largest province. Geographically, it is made up of three regions—the plateau-like highlands of the Canadian Shield in the north; the Appalachian Mountain region, which extends partly through the area south of the Saint Lawrence River; and the Saint Lawrence lowlands.

Quebec is a major producer of gold, iron ore, and copper. The Saint Lawrence lowlands are a fertile area where agriculture was once the mainstay of life. While agriculture is still important, it has been overtaken by high technology and manufacturing, especially textiles and clothing.

Quebec has a predominantly French-speaking population that boasts a culture all its own, setting it apart from the rest of Canada. The capital of Quebec is Quebec City, a city with an Old World European atmosphere. Montreal, Quebec's largest city, is a great industrial, commercial, and financial center.

ONTARIO Ontario includes portions of the Canadian Shield in the north and the Great Lakes-Saint Lawrence lowlands in the south. While Ontario's northern terrain is rugged and rocky, its lowlands support a dense and highly industrialized population that produces about 40 percent of Canada's gross domestic product.

The cluster of cities around the western end of Lake Ontario is known as Canada's golden horseshoe. It includes Oshawa, the center of Canada's automobile industry; Hamilton, the center of Canada's iron and steel manufacture; and Toronto.

Toronto is Canada's largest and most cosmopolitan city. The CN Tower, the tallest self-supporting structure in the world at 1,815 feet (553 m), dominates the skyline.

Ontario is Canada's wealthiest province, and about a third of Canada's population live there. Ontario is also the most ethnically diverse, with French and English mixing with many other Europeans, Asians, and Central Americans. Cosmopolitan Toronto, Ontario's capital, is Canada's largest city, and its financial and business center. Ottawa, near Ontario's southeastern border with Quebec, is the capital of Canada.

MANITOBA Northeastern Manitoba is part of the Canadian Shield, characterized by hills and forests; the southwestern part is flat.

The economy of Manitoba has been built on agriculture, mainly the growing of wheat and other grain crops. Winnipeg, the capital, is the industrial center of the province. It was the first stop in the great rush for land by European settlers who followed the railroad west, and is today home to their descendants—Ukrainian, Hungarian, Polish, Italian, and Portuguese Canadians.

A spectacular winter scene of the Lion's Gate Bridge in Vancouver in British Columbia.

SASKATCHEWAN Two-thirds of this great grain-producing province is flat, prairie lowland, where most of Canada's wheat crop is grown. In addition to grain, Saskatchewan's economy relies on cattle and hog farming, and softwood lumber harvesting. The province is also rich in mineral resources, especially potash (Saskatchewan is a major world producer of potash), oil, and metals, notably uranium.

Regina, the province's capital, and the city of Saskatoon are distribution centers of mainly agricultural products for the surrounding rural areas.

ALBERTA The westernmost of the prairie provinces, Alberta's southeastern region is a dry, treeless prairie. From the prairie, the land rises gradually until it meets the Rocky Mountains in the west.

Alberta holds 80 percent of the nation's petroleum and 90 percent of its natural gas reserves, and it produces large quantities of coal. Agriculture is also important, especially grain and livestock.

Edmonton is Alberta's capital and its largest city. Calgary is its second-largest city.

BRITISH COLUMBIA British Columbia, or BC, consists almost entirely of the Cordillera, a region of parallel mountain ranges that run in a north-south direction. In the eastern Rocky Mountains, which extend south into the United States, there is a continuous range of wall-like ridges carved by glaciation. The central area of the province consists of several mountain ranges, plateaus, and lake basins. In the west are the Coast Mountains. The Inside Passage and the Strait of Georgia, which separate the Queen Charlotte Islands and Vancouver Island from the mainland, together form one of the finest natural waterways in the world.

Vancouver is BC's largest city, a rapidly growing cosmopolitan center for immigrants from all over the world. Victoria, BC's capital and its second-largest city, is on the southern tip of Vancouver Island.

THE YUKON, NORTHWEST TERRITORIES, AND NUNAVUT The Yukon—which means great river in Athapaskan—is full of jagged mountains, boundless waterways, and sharp seasonal contrasts. The equally magnificent Northwest Territories, or NWT, occupy roughly 12 percent of Canada. Nunavut, a new territory, occupies 24 percent of the nation. Much of Nunavut is frozen arctic terrain.

Canada's highest mountain, Mount Logan, at 19,550 feet (5,959 m), is in the Yukon, while Canada's longest river, the Mackenzie, at 2,635 miles (4,241 km), is in the NWT. The capital cities are Whitehorse (the Yukon), Yellowknife (the NWT), and Iqualuit (Nunavut). The whole region is north of latitude 60°, and part of it is within the Arctic Circle. The Alaska Highway, which runs for 1,488 miles (2,395 km) from Dawson Creek in BC to Fairbanks in Alaska, provides the best road access to the Yukon.

This "signpost forest" at Watson's Lake in the Yukon contains contributions from all over the world.

Quebec City, one of the oldest cities in Canada, is situated on the Saint Lawrence River.

SAINT LAWRENCE SEAWAY The Saint Lawrence Seaway is a system of locks, canals, and channels that link the Great Lakes with the Atlantic Ocean. A monumental feat of engineering, the waterway extends 2,342 miles (3,769 km) from the Atlantic Ocean to the northern tip of Lake Superior. The waterway provides access to ocean-going ships from Montreal to Duluth, Minnesota, on Lake Superior.

The Montreal-Lake Ontario section, which is often thought of as the whole seaway, has four locks that together lift a ship traveling westward about 213 feet (65 m). Between Lake Ontario and Lake Erie, the Welland Canal circumvents Niagara Falls.

The cost of constructing the Saint Lawrence Seaway was shared by Canada and the United States. The two nations have co-managed the

A NEW TERRITORY

In 1999, for the first time since 1949, the map of Canada changed. The territory of Nunavut was created as part of a treaty settlement between the Inuit and the Canadian government. The territory, which includes two-thirds of the former NWT, or some 747,495 square miles (1,936,113 square km), is run by Canada's first aboriginal self-government. Nunavut means our land in Inuktitut, the Inuit language.

seaway since it opened in 1959. The seaway is vital to the Canadian economy, opening the interior of the continent to ocean-going ships and allowing direct, energy-efficient transportation of materials such as iron ore, grain, and coal.

COLD, HOT, WET, AND DRY

The climate in Canada varies considerably from region to region, from an arctic extreme where temperatures are below freezing most of the year, to the southern regions where the milder weather of spring, summer, and fall linger for at least eight months of the year.

Atlantic Canada has a fairly changeable climate. There is often a lot of snow in winter, and fog is common in spring and summer. Central Canada, from the Great Lakes to the Rocky Mountains, has a continental climate, with cold winters and hot summers and light, unreliable rainfall. Southern Ontario and Quebec, where the Great Lakes-Saint Lawrence lowlands are located, have cold winters with heavy snowfall and hot but fairly wet summers.

The northernmost region of the Northwest Territories offers awe-inspiring vistas of glaciers, cliffs, and fjords—all monuments of the Ice Age.

The climate is the most temperate on the western coast, where warm winds blowing from the Pacific Ocean keep winters mild, though cloudy and wet.

In the north, areas within the Arctic Circle experience extremely long, cold winters and only a few months with above-freezing temperatures.

Over the years Canadians have learned to live with and develop a healthy respect for their climate. When they are indoors, the marvels of central heating in winter and air conditioning in summer insulate them from the extremes of weather. Outdoors they know how to dress properly for protection against the cold and the sun.

FORESTS AND GRASSLANDS

Urbanization has greatly reduced Canada's extensive forest cover. Yet, around 45 percent of the country remains forested—from the northern frontiers to the outskirts of the largest cities.

Most of Canada's forests lie within the northern regions, stretching from Newfoundland to the Yukon and extending into western Canada on the slopes of the Rockies and parallel mountain ranges. These forests consist mainly of evergreens and conifers such as fir, spruce, and pine.

Temperate forests of broad-leaved deciduous trees, such as oak, maple, elm, beech, and ash, which shed their leaves in the fall, are found in the milder, southern parts of the country. On the western coast, the mild and wet climate supports the growth of dense forests of tall trees such as the Douglas fir, Sitka spruce, and western red cedar. The Douglas fir is Canada's tallest tree species, growing to on average more than 200 feet (60 m).

In the interior, with light rainfall and a high evaporation rate, grasses range in height from 6 inches (15 cm) to 8 feet (2.5 m). The grasslands of Canada's interior cover most of the prairie provinces and the drier areas of the interior of British Columbia. The grasses have adapted to the dry climate. Their abundant roots readily absorb moisture, which is then conserved in their narrow leaves, and their slender, flexible stalks bend with the wind.

In the coldest parts of the country, the arctic and alpine regions, there are tundra meadows of coarse grasses, mosses, and lichens. Few trees grow here because of the severe climate.

The evergreen forest of Banff National Park in Alberta is Canada's first national park, created in 1885.

THE GREAT AND THE SMALL

The wildlife of Canada is extremely diverse and varies dramatically from region to region, from the pygmy shrew, Canada's smallest mammal, growing to around 3 inches (75 mm) in length and weighing less than an ounce, to the blue whale, the largest known creature, growing up to 100 feet (30 m) in length and weighing 150 tons.

Animals in Canada have adapted to the cold winters. Some migrate south in the fall, some grow a thick winter coat of fur or feathers, and others hibernate, living off a thick layer of fat accumulated during the warmer seasons.

The inland waters and the seas in Canada support teeming colonies of microscopic plankton and the large number of fish, amphibians, and marine mammals that feed on plankton.

Canada geese can reach a wingspan of up to 6.6 feet (2 m). The birds nest and breed in Canada, then fly south in winter.

The grasslands support herbivores, such as deer and elk, while the forests provide food and shelter for rabbits, squirrels, and rodents. Birds of prey such as hawks and eagles stay in Canada throughout the year, while other birds, such as insect eaters, fly south in winter.

Human colonization has caused the extinction of many species of animals in Canada. Some, such as the Dawson caribou, the sea mink, and a penguin-like bird called the great auk have been hunted to extinction. Others, such as the greater prairie chicken, have declined in number because of the destruction of their natural habitat.

Amid growing environmental concern in Canada, strict hunting regulations and conservation efforts are turning the tide. Animal species such as the musk oxen, whooping crane, and bald eagle are protected by law. There were once fewer than 1,000 musk oxen and American bison in Canada, but the protection of the law has brought them back from the verge of extinction.

CANADA'S BEARS

Three types of bears can be found in Canada. The most familiar is the black bear, which can be found almost anywhere in the country except in the extreme north.

Black bears, which are sometimes brown in color, are good climbers. They are omnivores and will eat almost anything they can find. Vegetation forms a large part of their diet, especially berries and nuts in summer. Bears may become accustomed to scavenging for food in garbage dumps. This brings them into close contact with people. Black bears are normally shy animals, but those that have developed the habit of feeding on garbage sometimes become a nuisance and a danger to people.

The grizzly bear is found in western Alberta, British Columbia, the Yukon, the Northwest Territories, and Nunavut. It is much larger than the black bear and has a characteristic hump over the shoulders formed by the muscles of its forelegs. It gets its name from the light or grizzled fur on its head and shoulders. The grizzly is also omnivorous, often digging for roots, but it will prey on elk, moose, deer, and caribou as well.

Polar bears inhabit the arctic sea coast. They vary in color from almost pure white in winter to a yellow or golden color in summer and the fall. Their thick winter coats and a thick layer of fat under the skin protect them from the cold. They are more carnivorous than the grizzly or black bear, preying mostly on seals.

TIME ZONES

Before 1884 local time in Canada was determined by setting noon as the moment when the sun was directly overhead. But that moment was reached at different times in different parts of the country, and that made local time vary considerably across Canada. The time difference was not a problem until railroads made it possible for people to travel relatively quickly over long distances. The traditional method of calculating local time made it difficult to work out train schedules. A Canadian Pacific Railway surveyor, Sir Sandford Fleming, came up with the time zone system. It works by using a standard or mean time to fix the variation of time within established time zones.

Sir Fleming's system was first used by the North American railway systems in 1883. Today, Canada has six time zones. They are, from east to west, Newfoundland, Atlantic, Eastern, Central, Mountain, and Pacific Standard. The difference between each time zone is one hour, except between Atlantic Standard Time and Newfoundland Standard Time, where the difference is half an hour.

In 1918 Daylight Saving Time gave Canadians an extra hour of daylight each day in summer. On the first Sunday in April, clocks are put forward one hour, and on the last Sunday in October, clocks are reset to Standard Time.

Canada's six time zones: the hours indicated in each shows how many hours the zone is behind Greenwich Mean Time.

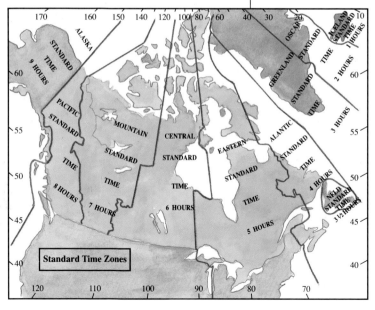

Standard Time Zones

HISTORY

CANADA'S HISTORY is one of immigration and settlement. The 10 provinces and three territories extending from the Atlantic to the Pacific oceans are home to peoples whose ancestors came from many lands.

While there have been no great wars of independence or civil strife, Canadians have over time struggled with nature and with differences among themselves to create a nation. Nevertheless, some tensions remain unresolved even today.

EARLY SETTLERS

Most anthropologists agree that Canada's first inhabitants crossed the Bering Strait from Asia more than 25,000 years ago during the Ice Age. They came over a land bridge that then joined Asia and North America. These first immigrants were nomads who traveled the land hunting animals for food. As the weather warmed and the ice melted, animals and people moved south into the heart of North America. Eventually, people learned to gather wild plants and cultivate the rich soil. They stopped wandering and became the first settlers of the land.

Canada's early peoples evolved into many different cultural and linguistic groups. The groups varied as widely as the terrain and gave themselves names such as Dené, Nahani, and Kutchin, which simply meant the people. European explorers who came looking for a western route to India called them Indians.

Despite their cultural and linguistic diversity, Canada's first settlers shared a deep, spiritual relationship with the land and with nature. But when the Europeans arrived, they brought conflict and diseases that caused devastation among the indigenous peoples. For decades, the indigenous population of Canada declined, threatening the existence of the land's unique cultures.

Formerly referred to as Indians, the indigenous peoples of Canada have adopted the names First Peoples and First Nations. Unlike in the United States, where the term Native American is common, the indigenous peoples of Canada are usually referred to informally as natives.

Opposite: **Totem poles in Stanley Park, Vancouver, British Columbia.**

INDIGENOUS GROUPS

Nomads in the interior plains hunted bison for meat and skins. They included the Blackfoot, Blood, Piegan, Gros Ventre, Plains Cree, Sioux, and Assiniboin. Families lived in groups in tepees, which were conical tents covered with skins. The portable tepees were easy to erect and dismantle yet warm and stable enough to withstand winds.

Groups on the western coast, such as the Haida, Tsimshian, Nootka, Coast Salish, Kwakiutl (kwa-ki-yud-l), and Bella Coola, established permanent villages and lived from the bounty of the sea, fishing for salmon and hunting whales. They built large houses from cedar and carved tall totem poles and other objects from cedar and stone.

The nomadic woodland peoples in the east—the Algonkians, Mi'kmaq, Montagnais, Naskapi, Ojibway, and Cree—lived in lodges and wigwams constructed of poles, bark, and skins. They were hunters and trappers who followed migratory animals.

The Iroquoian hunters of southern Ontario—the Huron, Tobacco Nation, Neutrals, Mohawk, Oneida, Onondaga, Cayuga, Seneca, and Tuscarora—were superb farmers. They grew corn, beans, and squash and lived in permanent villages of longhouses.

The peoples of the interior plateau were the Interior Salish, Kutenai, Chilcotin, Carrier, and Tagish who hunted and fished for food. Their dwellings ranged from subterranean pits to bison-hide tepees.

The indigenous people of the far north were the Inuit, meaning the people. They hunted caribou, whales, and seals. They lived in snow houses called igloos that protected them from the cold. Inside the igloo, a small oil lamp, and body heat, kept people comfortably warm.

Warm in winter and cool in summer, the tepee is able to withstand gale-force winds and yet is easily dismantled for travel.

ARRIVAL OF THE EUROPEANS

Archeological evidence shows that in A.D. 1000 a Viking adventurer, Leif Ericsson, established a colony on the island of Newfoundland. It lasted only a few years. For centuries after the Vikings, there was very little European exploration of the new continent, until the search for a new sea route to the East led to the discovery of America by Christopher Columbus.

When news of the vastness and riches of the new land reached Europe, it attracted many European adventurers such as John Cabot. He briefly explored the waters around Newfoundland and Labrador in 1497 and returned to England with news of rich fishing grounds.

The indigenous peoples remained relatively unaffected until the first colonizers, the French adventurers and explorers, arrived. One of them was Giovanni di Verrazano, who in the employment of the King of France landed in Newfoundland in 1524 and claimed it for France.

The most northerly Inuit traditionally lived in igloos made from ice blocks in winter and tents made of skins in summer.

"Now, God be praised, I will die in peace," said the dying James Wolfe to his officers on the Plains of Abraham.

FRENCH-ENGLISH RIVALRY

In the early stages of the struggle for control of the new continent, the French outdid the English. French soldiers, missionaries, adventurous fur traders called *coureurs de bois* (koo-rer de BWAH), meaning runners of the woods, and explorers such as Jacques Cartier and Samuel de Champlain opened up North America.

The French were lured by the belief that the land they had discovered was rich in gold. They were also driven by the idea of bringing salvation and civilization to the "savages" of the land, and they hoped to gain new land and glory for their king. But instead of gold, they found something nearly as valuable—a large supply of fur, especially beaver pelts.

By the 1670s, New France, the empire in North America, reached from as far north as the Hudson Bay in the Arctic to the Gulf of Mexico in the south. It was run on a seigneurial system, which means that the French settlers were granted land by the French Crown in return for services. The *seigneurs* then subdivided the land to rent it out to other settlers, called *habitants*, who farmed the land. No more than 10,000 immigrants came to settle during the entire history of New France. Yet they prospered, growing to a population of 60,000 by 1760.

EMPIRE BUILDER

In 1534 French explorer and navigator Jacques Cartier sailed into the Gulf of Saint Lawrence and landed on the Gaspé Peninsula. Planting a great cross, he claimed the land for France and for God. In 1535 Cartier made his second voyage up the Saint Lawrence River to the site of present-day Montreal. He became the first European to enter the Canadian interior. On his third voyage to the new land, in 1541, Cartier established a settlement, but this colony lasted only until 1543. Cartier and many other French explorers helped build a vast empire in North America called New France.

COUREURS DE BOIS

"We were Caesars, being nobody to contradict us," said French explorer and trader Pierre-Esprit Radisson in 1661 describing the life of the *coureurs de bois*, the backbone of the early trading system.

The *coureurs de bois* were bold, boisterous adventurers who trapped animals while living a precarious existence in the wild. Many had come from France to escape a life of drudgery. Some had exchanged prison sentences for emigration papers.

"I am happy that I shall not live to see the surrender of Quebec," were among the last words of the Marquis de Montcalm.

Pressure on New France came from English settlements to the east and south, because French-controlled lands blocked the westward expansion of the English colonies on the eastern seaboard. In the north, the French faced rivalry from the Hudson's Bay Company for dominance of the fur trade. As a result, New France and the English fought an almost continuous series of battles in the 17th and 18th centuries in which the indigenous communities allied themselves with one side or the other.

The end of New France came in 1759 with the fall of the city of Quebec in which British sea power played an important role. The British navy, controlling the Atlantic, cut the colony of New France off from the mother country. With troops on board commanded by England's youngest general, 32-year-old James Wolfe, a British fleet sailed down the Saint Lawrence River for Quebec. The battle raged for months, climaxing on the Plains of Abraham, west of the city. Wolfe's men

General Montcalm after the French defeat at the Battle of Quebec in 1759.

formed their famous "thin red line" across the plains, while French forces, under the command of Marquis de Montcalm, advanced. After the battle, the Plains of Abraham were covered with the fallen French. Both commanders were mortally wounded. Wolfe lived just long enough to learn he had won, while Montcalm died a few hours later. In 1763 France ceded its North American territories to Britain through the Treaty of Paris.

An old cannon from the French-Indian Wars, facing out into the Saint Lawrence River from the Château Coteau du Lac in Quebec.

INVASION AND IMMIGRATION

The new imperial rulers found themselves masters of a population that was different in language and religion. To prevent an uprising, Governor Sir Guy Carleton concluded that French civil and religious rights had to be upheld. In the Quebec Act of 1774, legal status was given to the Roman Catholic Church, to the seigneurial system of landholding, and to French civil law.

When the colonists in North America revolted against British rule in the mid-1770s, Quebec was expected to join the uprising. But that did not happen because the French, who were staunch Royalists and Catholics, had little love for the Protestant republicans in the south. America gained independence, but Britain still reigned supreme in the north.

The American Revolution had a dramatic side effect. Thousands of Americans who had been faithful to England migrated north. Most of these United Empire Loyalists populated the mainly empty shores of Nova Scotia, creating a new colony called New Brunswick, while others settled along the northern shore of Lake Ontario.

The new British settlers soon changed the way Canada was governed. Being accustomed to representative institutions, the Loyalists chafed under French seigneurial and civil law. To avoid conflict, in 1791 Britain created two colonies, Upper and Lower Canada. Upper Canada was controlled by Loyalist elements, while Lower Canada, with the city of Quebec as its center, remained essentially French in character.

Meanwhile, antagonism grew between British North America and the United States, culminating in the War of 1812. Failure by the British to withdraw from American territories was one reason for the conflict.

Another reason was Britain's war with France. Britain prevented American ships from trading with France and forced sailors aboard these ships into its services. In 1812 an American army marched up the banks of the Richelieu River, only to be pushed back by British forces. It was the only time that Canada and the United States fought each other. After several skirmishes in which neither side won, the war ended with the Treaty of Ghent in 1814. Britain and the United States agreed to demilitarize the Great Lakes and extend the border along the 49th parallel to the Rockies.

After the war, the British government, in an effort to strengthen the colonies, helped immigrants to settle in British North America. Others came of their own accord, fleeing the poverty of the early stages of the Industrial Revolution, the starvation wages in bleak factory towns, and an impoverished life on farms. From 1815 to 1855, a million Europeans arrived at the ports of Halifax, Saint John, and Quebec. They changed the ethnic composition of the country, making the French-speaking population the minority.

In Lower Canada, the French showed their discontent with several uprisings against British domination. The rebellion of 1837 brought Lord Durham from Britain to investigate the cause of the political unrest. He recommended that the two provinces be joined once again into a united Province of Canada. Durham thought unity was the best way to increase Canada's economic progress, the way unification had in the United States. The Province of Canada was created in 1841.

Halifax in Nova Scotia was a popular place for immigrants to settle in the 19th century.

THE HUDSON'S BAY COMPANY

The green, red, yellow, and blue stripes of The Bay department store are prominent in the shopping centers of many towns and cities in Canada. The department store is the modern format of a more-than-300-year-old company. The Hudson's Bay Company is the oldest incorporated joint-stock merchandising company in the English-speaking world. It played a very important role in the opening up of Canada, especially in the northern and western parts of the country. It was originally a fur trading company that had its base in Hudson's Bay in the north. From there it exploited the interior of the continent.

In 1670 King Charles II of England signed a royal charter granting the "Governor and Company of Adventurers" wide powers, including exclusive trading rights in the vast territory called Rupert's Land, where the rivers flowed into Hudson Bay. The company fought with the French for control of the fur trade until 1713 when France acknowledged England's claim to Hudson Bay in the Treaty of Utrecht. In 1821 the Hudson's Bay Company extended its monopoly to the west when it merged with its former rival, the North West Company. For almost two centuries, the company not only controlled the fur trade but effectively ruled the land, being responsible for providing law and order and government in the region. When it sold Rupert's Land to Canada in 1870, the company retained much of the land on which it had its trading posts and large areas of the prairies. It became increasingly involved in real estate, at the same time doing much business with settlers through the trading posts it had retained.

The Hudson's Bay Company's main competitor was the North West Company, founded in 1783 and established in Manitoba. Conflict between the two trading rivals occasionally broke out, leading to killings on both sides. In 1821, in an attempt to diffuse hostilities, the British government merged the two under the Hudson's Bay Company.

THE MÉTIS OF MANITOBA

The Métis are a people created by the union of French and Scottish trappers with indigenous women. They were originally hunters and trackers who lived a seminomadic way of life hunting bison. But bison dwindled as the railroad opened up the west. Afraid that their rights might be ignored, the Métis, under their charismatic leader Louis Riel, revolted and forced the federal government to grant provincial status to Manitoba. Peace was restored for a while, but in 1885 the Métis rebelled again. This time they were crushed, and Riel was executed. In 2003 an Ontario court ruled that the Métis in the province deserved the same rights as other indigenous communities in Canada, as had been promised but not practiced in Section 35 of the 1982 Constitution Act.

THE BIRTH OF A NATION

The colonies of New Brunswick, Nova Scotia, Prince Edward Island, and Newfoundland and Labrador initially had little to do with the Province of Canada. They attracted their share of settlers from Europe. The colonies were directly controlled by the government in London. The 1840s and 1850s were a period of rapid change. Britain adopted a free-trade policy and granted the provinces self-government in local matters. That caused the colonies to develop closer economic ties with the United States.

In 1864 after the leaders of the three maritime provinces of Nova Scotia, New Brunswick, and Prince Edward Island had decided to discuss the possibility of unification of the three provinces, the Province of Canada took it as an opportunity to present a grander proposal—the union of all five into a large country, Canada. The political situation after the American Civil War in the 1860s had much to do with the birth of the new nation. The increased threat that the American army might turn its attention to the British colonies in the north coupled with Britain's desire to see its colonies take more responsibility for domestic affairs cemented the plan.

In 1866 the provinces of Nova Scotia, New Brunswick, and Canada sent delegates to England to present their proposal to the British parliament. Once an agreement was reached, the parliament passed the British North America Act, which came into effect on July 1, 1867, creating the Dominion of Canada. The provinces of Manitoba, British Columbia, Prince Edward Island, Alberta, Saskatchewan, and Newfoundland and Labrador joined the union later.

The word Canada is derived from the Huron-Iroquois word "kanata," which means village.

A WORLD POWER

After Confederation, Canada continued to attract large numbers of immigrants who filled the cities and farmed the land. The country's products, such as wheat, paper, timber, and minerals, were supplied to an international market, making the country prosperous in the early decades of the 20th century.

Despite Confederation, domestic politics were dominated for many years by the issue of francophone (French-speaking) rights outside of Quebec. The sensitive issue flared again and divided Canadians deeply during World War I when the federal government decided that it had to boost the country's military ranks with enforced conscription.

French Canadians were violently opposed to the decision, seeing it as a move to reduce their already declining numbers. Canadian unity was strained almost to the breaking point. The war took a heavy toll, as more

Men of the Canadian 48th Highlanders in action in Europe in 1944.

The war memorial in Ottawa commemorates those who died in the two world wars.

than 60,000 Canadians died in battle. However, when hostilities ended, industrial development accelerated and the economy again prospered. New resources such as lead and zinc and new products such as automobiles and radios found expanding markets both at home and abroad.

The Great Depression of the 1930s hit Canada hard, causing one financial crisis after another, until the outbreak of World War II. Canada provided munitions and food supplies to the Allied war effort, and Canadian troops played a major role in defeating enemy forces in Italy and in the Allied landings at Normandy, France. Some 42,000 Canadians were killed during World War II.

The expansion of the economy due to the war effort helped Canada to join the ranks of global industrialized powers. Postwar immigration doubled Canada's population and provided labor for the new industries that developed all over the country.

Today, Canada has emerged as a major world power and is ranked among the most affluent nations in the world. Politically and economically, Canada and the United States have developed very close relations.

HISTORY OF ABORIGINAL POLICY

Unlike in the United States, where the wild West and its cowboys and Indians were very much part of American history, there was little or no hostility between the indigenous peoples and the European settlers in Canada. From the very beginning, both the British and French were interested in getting local cooperation in their fur trade. Then, as the Europeans became interested in working the land, they sought to take the land from the indigenous peoples, not through war but through a series of treaty agreements.

An indigenous Canadian lists his demands on his T-shirt.

Through these agreements, the indigenous peoples surrendered their rights to the land in return for special reserve lands that were set aside entirely for their use. Between 1764 and 1862 several treaties were signed, mostly covering the fertile agricultural lands on Lake Ontario's northern shore. After Confederation, between 1871 and 1921, another 11 treaties opened up land for new settlers from coast to coast.

The Indian Act of 1876 gave the government great powers to control indigenous peoples living on reserves, generally by governing all aspects of their lives in the hope that eventually they would become assimilated with the rest of society. Even when it was revised in 1951, the Indian Act was still very restrictive. It distinguished between status and non-status Indians, that is, those who were registered with the government as Indians and those who were not, and discriminated against indigenous women by taking away their Indian status if they did not marry an indigenous man. Through a government residential school system, indigenous

QUEBEC SEPARATISM

Separatism is the advocacy of separation or secession by a group from a larger political unit to which it belongs.

In Canada the term is associated with the aspirations of the French-speaking people of Quebec, who see separatism as the means of stopping the decline of their culture and language in a continent that is English-dominated. This philosophy is embodied by the political party Parti Québécois, which was formed in 1968. The party is committed to a program of sovereignty-association, that is, it espouses political independence from Canada while retaining some links, such as a common currency. Popular support for the Parti Québécois resulted in the party being swept to power in 1976 and again in 1981. Yet, in 1980, when asked in a province-wide referendum whether they would support sovereignty-association negotiations with the rest of Canada, the people of Quebec said no.

During the constitutional crisis of 1992, Canadians as a whole and the people of Quebec themselves rejected a new constitutional accord that had been put together by their political leaders. This raised the specter of separatism once again. However, in a 1995 referendum the people of Quebec voted to remain a part of Canada. The separatist movement in Quebec has since faltered somewhat, but only time will tell if Canada remains intact.

children were forcibly taken away from their families in order to push the process of assimilation. From the late 1940s indigenous leaders had spoken out against this policy and expressed their people's desire to regain their rightful position of equality with Canadians of other races. Accordingly, in 1970 the government began helping indigenous groups and associations research the treaties and first peoples rights.

In 1972 the National Indian Brotherhood, now the Assembly of First Nations, asked that the first peoples be given control over their own education, so that their children could learn their culture. The proposal was adopted in 1973 by the Department of Indian Affairs and Northern Development. The Canadian government also announced its willingness to consider first peoples' claims. This need to discuss indigenous rights and titles to land, resources, and self-government continues today.

GOVERNMENT

CANADA IS, GEOGRAPHICALLY, the second largest democratic country in the world. It is a constant challenge to make democracy work in a country so large and populated with people of such diverse backgrounds.

When on July 1, 1867, Canada became a nation, it also became a democratic federation. The powers of government are shared between a central or federal government and the governments of the various provinces that make up the nation. The Constitution Act of 1867, also called the British North America Act of 1867, established one parliament for Canada consisting of the British monarch, the senate, and the House of Commons.

THE BRITISH CROWN AND ITS REPRESENTATIVES

Queen Elizabeth II of Great Britain is the official head of state, which makes Canada a constitutional monarchy. The monarch is represented in Canada by a governor-general, who has no political power. The prime minister is the head of government. The queen can protect the parliament and the people against any abuse of powers by the prime minister and the cabinet.

Canada's parliamentary system, based on the British parliament, was set up in 1867. Sir John A. Macdonald was the first prime minister and Charles Stanley, the Baron Monck, the first governor-general of the newly formed Dominion of Canada. Originally all the governor-generals came from England. The first Canadian-born person to hold the position was Vincent Massey in 1952. His successor, Georges Philias Vanier, became the first French-Canadian governor-general in 1959. In 1984 Jeanne Sauvé became the first woman governor-general. The present and 26th governor-general, the Right Honourable Adrienne Clarkson, is the second woman and the first Chinese-Canadian to occupy the position.

Opposite: **The eastern block of the parliament building in Ottawa. Before it stands a statue of Sir Wilfrid Laurier (1841–1919), the first Canadian prime minister of French ancestry, who governed from 1896 to 1911.**

Queen Elizabeth II, queen of England and head of the Commonwealth since 1952.

DUTIES OF THE GOVERNOR-GENERAL

The governor-general is appointed for five years. He or she has no real political power and is not involved in party politics. The governor-general gives "royal assent" to acts of parliament; signs state documents; appoints the leader of the party in power as prime minister; opens, discontinues, or dissolves the parliament on the advice of the prime minister; and reads the "speech from the throne" at the opening of a new parliament and at every new session of parliament.

One of the most important duties of a governor-general is to ensure that the nation is never leaderless. In the event that the prime minister dies or resigns suddenly, the governor-general will appoint a temporary prime minister to lead the nation until a new leader is chosen.

IS THE MONARCHY STILL RELEVANT?

At the end of the 20th century, when asked which symbols they considered important to their nation, Canadians put the monarchy far down on the list. Nevertheless, the British royal family still has a strong hold on the imagination of the people. A visit by any member of the British royalty to Canada is always enthusiastically welcomed, and their doings, scandalous or otherwise, are closely followed in Canada.

THE SENATE

The senate was formed in 1867. It has two roles. First, the composition of the senate is based on regional representation to ensure that Canada's linguistic minorities, such as Quebec's French speakers, are adequately taken care of.

Second, the senate reviews laws passed by the House of Commons. The senate receives proposed laws in the form of a bill from the House of Commons and either passes the bill with or without making amendments to it, so that the bill then becomes law, or rejects it.

The 105-seat senate occasionally has vacancies due to retirement and death. In 2003 there were 103 members—24 each from Quebec and Ontario; 10 from New Brunswick; nine from Nova Scotia; six each from British Columbia, Manitoba, Saskatchewan, and Newfoundland and Labrador; five from Alberta; four from Prince Edward Island; and one each from the Yukon, the Northwest Territories, and Nunavut.

Senators are appointed by the governor-general in the queen's name, on the advice of the prime minister. Senators have to retire when they reach 75 years of age. To qualify as a senator, one must be a Canadian citizen at least 30 years old, reside in the province for which he or she is appointed, and own property worth at least $4,000 in that province and at least another $4,000 of personal property after debts and liabilities.

Pierre Trudeau, prime minister of Canada in 1968–79 and 1980–84.

THE HOUSE OF COMMONS

The House of Commons consists of elected representatives from all over the country. Known as Members of Parliament, the representatives come from various political parties and are elected by the people to speak on their behalf.

Representation in the House of Commons is based on population. There are now 301 Members of Parliament: 103 from Ontario, 75 from Quebec, 34 from British Columbia, 26 from Alberta, 14 each from Manitoba and Saskatchewan, 11 from Nova Scotia, 10 from New Brunswick, seven from Newfoundland, four from Prince Edward Island, and one each from the Yukon, the Northwest Territories, and Nunavut. The number of seats for each province is adjusted every 10 years following changes in population size.

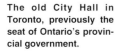

The old City Hall in Toronto, previously the seat of Ontario's provincial government.

The Members of Parliament meet in the House of Commons to discuss social, economic, and political issues and debate and pass laws. Another function of the House of Commons is to control the finances of the country through budget and taxation policies.

THE FEDERAL GOVERNMENT Canada's constitution requires that a new government be formed every five years, if not sooner. The governor-general dissolves the parliament and calls for an election. The leader of the winning political party is usually appointed prime minister, and he or she then appoints other elected Members of Parliament to form the cabinet.

Each province is usually represented by at least one cabinet minister. The cabinet is the policy-forming body of the government. Most cabinet ministers are assigned to one or more government departments, and they are responsible for formulating the policies of their departments. The actual work of putting these policies into practice is done by the civil service.

Paul Martin, the current Liberal Party leader, became prime minister upon the retirement of the party's former leader, Jean Chrétien, in December 2003.

THE OPPOSITION The political party with the second largest number of Members of Parliament forms the official opposition, Her Majesty's Loyal Opposition, to the government.

The opposition performs a very important role in government. It has the responsibility of checking and criticizing government proposals and policies and suggesting ways to improve the governing of the country. But the opposition must also present sound alternative policies and solutions of its own.

THE CONSTITUTION

Canada's constitution dates back to the British North America Act (1867). That act brought about the birth of the nation of Canada. But because it was an act of the British parliament, the Canadian government had to go to Britain to amend the act.

In 1982 the British parliament, at the Canadian government's request, passed the Canada Act. That had two significant consequences. First, it included in the constitution the Constitution Act of 1982. Second, it transfered Canada's legislative authority from Great Britain to Canada.

Today, Canada's constitution has four main features. First, it establishes Canada both as a constitutional monarchy and a parliamentary democracy. Second, it makes Canada a confederation with power divided between the federal and provincial levels of government.

The other two features are new. The new act nationalized the constitution and brought it home to Canada, and it established the Canadian Charter of Rights and Freedoms.

Former Parti Québécois leader Jacques Parizeau raises his arms in victory after the rejection of the constitutional accord by Canadian voters in 1992. Parizeau resigned soon after the 1995 Quebec referendum, when Quebecers voted against separation from the rest of Canada.

CONSTITUTIONAL CRISIS When a historic agreement was reached in November 1981 between the federal and provincial governments that cleared the way for the proclamation of the Constitution Act of 1982, only the province of Quebec withheld its agreement.

Since the act forms the basis of relations between the federal and provincial governments, the entire patriation of the constitution depends on an agreement by all provinces. The federal and provincial governments have been trying for many years to agree on such a formula. In 1987 the ministers met at Meech Lake to produce an accord that had to be ratified within three years. But by 1990 both Manitoba and Newfoundland and Labrador had failed to ratify the accord, and it floundered.

In a 1992 referendum, Canadians rejected a constitutional agreement known as the Charlottetown Accord. Things came to a head in 1995 when Parti Québécois leader Jacques Parizeau called for a referendum to allow Quebecers to decide once and for all whether they wanted to remain a part of Canada. The margin was close—49.4 percent for separation, 50.6 percent against.

Further attempts at resolving the crisis have also failed. As a result, Quebec remains the only province that has not signed the constitution under which it effectively operates.

CHARTER OF RIGHTS AND FREEDOMS

Every Canadian has fundamental rights and freedoms that are guaranteed by the Charter of Rights and Freedoms, as contained in the Constitution Act of 1982.

The charter guarantees all Canadians freedom of religion, thought, belief, opinion, and expression, including freedom of the press, freedom of peaceful assembly, and freedom of association.

It protects a Canadian citizen's mobility rights (to live, work, and move to wherever he or she chooses), legal rights (to life, liberty, and security), and equality rights (so that it is an offence to discriminate on the basis of race, origin, color, religion, gender, age, or disability).

It recognizes English and French as the two official languages of Canada and guarantees minority language educational rights, that is, a person's right, if in an English- or French-speaking minority, to be taught in his or her own language.

It is important, however, to realize that the charter expresses basic principles and that it may be difficult to determine a person's exact rights. It is therefore up to lawyers and judges to interpret charter rights and freedoms in accordance with the law and with specific case circumstances.

OTTAWA, SEAT OF GOVERNMENT

In the mid-19th century, when Upper and Lower Canada were joined to form the Province of Canada, there was such rivalry between the two provinces that neither Toronto nor Montreal could serve as the capital. Instead, the legislative branch had to meet alternately in both cities.

When looking for the site of the new capital, Queen Victoria selected the provincial town of Ottawa (which was formerly known as Bytown, named after Colonel By who constructed the Rideau Canal that cuts through the city) as a compromise, because Ottawa was located on the border between Upper and Lower Canada. Sir Edmund Head, then the governor-general, remarked: "I believe that the least objectionable place is the city of Ottawa. Every city is jealous of every other city except Ottawa." Ottawa thus became the capital of the Dominion of Canada in 1867.

ABORIGINAL SELF-GOVERNMENT

In 1982, because of problems caused by the Indian Act and increasing demands by the first peoples for more power and a better standard of living, a special committee on aboriginal self-government was created.

In 1983 the committee recommended that the government establish with the First Nations people a new relationship in which self-government was an essential element.

Accordingly, the Canadian government has committed itself to seeing that the principle of self-government is entrenched in the constitution. Discussions are held regularly on exactly how new laws can facilitate the transfer of a wide range of powers to the various indigenous nations.

ROYAL CANADIAN MOUNTED POLICE

The Mountie in his scarlet coat is familiar to people around the world as an icon of Canada. The Mountie stands as a symbol of law and order and authority to all Canadians.

When the Canadian government took over control of the vast territories under the Hudson's Bay Company, it realized that something would have to be done to prevent the western and northern wilderness from degenerating into the lawlessness that had accompanied much of the opening of the American West. In 1873 the parliament passed an act that established a temporary police force for the territories. One hundred and fifty recruits were sent that winter to Fort Garry in Manitoba, followed by another 150 later in spring.

The new police force, named the North-West Mounted Police, was organized along the lines of a cavalry regiment, armed with guns and dressed much like soldiers, in scarlet tunics and blue trousers, to stress their symbolic link with the British army. The new force set up a network of police posts and patrolled the land, effectively curbing the lawlessness of adventurers, many of whom had come from the United States. When gold was discovered in the Klondike, the North-West Mounted Police were immediately sent into the Yukon. Their presence ensured that the Klondike gold rush became the most orderly gold rush in history.

By the early 20th century, Canadians had begun to realize that the mounted police were here to stay. The Canadian government decided in 1919 to expand the Royal North-West Mounted Police, as it was then known, into a national police force.

When the legislation took effect in 1920, the mounted police headquarters were moved from Regina to Ottawa, and they became known as the Royal Canadian Mounted Police and gradually took over policing duties all over the country.

Today, a member of the RCMP wears a blue uniform. The scarlet tunic worn by Mounties as popularized in books and movies is in fact worn only on special occasions. But whether in red or blue, uniformed Mounties are on-duty police officers.

At that time, there was nothing else in favor of Ottawa as the capital. Essayist Goldwin Smith called the city a "sub-Arctic lumber village, converted by royal mandate into a political cockpit." Today, however, Ottawa is living up to its name as the seat of the Canadian government. It is a modern city with a population of more than 1.2 million, and it is located at the confluence of three rivers in a beautiful setting that is enhanced by the National Capital Commission with parks and sidewalks lined with flowers.

ECONOMY

CANADA'S RICH NATURAL RESOURCES have from the earliest times provided for Canadians their basic needs, such as food, clothing, and shelter. It was Canada's natural wealth that attracted the first European settlers and traders who came and worked the land. Natural resources remain the backbone of an increasingly diversified and industrialized Canadian economy.

AGRICULTURE

In earlier times, most Canadians were farmers. There was a lot of subsistence farming, and farmers sold their produce in the domestic market. This picture has changed dramatically. Today, less than 2 percent of the population is engaged in agricultural activity. Despite this low percentage, the average farm is much larger in size than it once was and, thanks to technological advances, can produce much more than before.

Slightly more than half of what Canada produces is exported. The importance of agriculture to the economy is reflected in the assistance farmers receive from the government. There are programs to regulate and promote agricultural education and research and development. Farmers raise livestock and grow grain, fruit, vegetables, and other crops.

The prairie regions of Manitoba, Saskatchewan, and Alberta, home to almost all of Canada's farmland, produce grain and support a large beef-cattle industry. Saskatchewan produces much of Canada's wheat, and Alberta is the chief producer of feed-grain and beef cattle. Potatoes are the main crop in Prince Edward Island. Quebec is the world's largest producer of maple syrup.

Above: **Grain storage in Manitoba.**

Opposite: **The port of Sault Ste. Marie, Ontario, along the busy Saint Lawrence Seaway.**

Forestry products are a highly lucrative source of income for Canada.

FORESTRY

Forests cover 45 percent of Canada, or about 10 percent of the world's total forest area. About 1.6 million square miles (4.18 million square km) of forested land consist mainly of coniferous trees, much of which is publicly owned. Forests are an integral part of Canada's tradition, culture, and history. The health of the forest sector affects the economy of every province from Newfoundland and Labrador on the Atlantic Ocean to British Columbia on the Pacific Ocean.

One in 17 jobs is linked directly or indirectly to the nation's forests. Forestry activities include logging and paper and pulp processing. The wood industry manufactures a wide range of products, from lumber and plywood to furniture and prefabricated building materials. Canada exports most of these products, mainly to the United States.

FOREST MANAGEMENT As the health and sustainability of the forests are vital to Canada's economy, the forest industry tries to strike a balance between satisfying the demand for wood and protecting biodiversity and the people's way of life.

Almost as many trees are destroyed each year by fire, pests, and disease as are harvested commercially. Provincial forestry agencies are responsible for seeing that the loss of trees is reduced. Thus, thinning, pruning, and clearing of forests is part of provincial forest management. Reforestation is also an important aspect of forest management. Millions of trees are replanted each year as part of forest renewal.

Logging is controversial, because the forest directly affects climate and is home to a large number of animals and plants. Canadian forestry faces a lot of opposition from conservationists, environmentalists, and First Nations, who claim that loggers often encroach on sacred grounds.

Opposition to logging affects the timber and retail industries alike. Campaigns that dissuade shoppers from patronizing stores selling old-growth wood products have led to falling sales, while loggers lose their jobs when logging areas come under government protection.

Lobster traps on a pier side in Nova Scotia, one of Canada's main fishing regions.

FISHING

Bordered on three sides by water and containing thousands of rivers and lakes, Canada has historically been one of the world's largest exporters of fish products. In 2002 Canada exported 75 percent of its fish production. More than half of those exports went to the United States, Japan, and the European Union. Canada's main fish exports are cod, herring, crab, lobster, shrimp, and scallops from the Atlantic coast, and halibut and salmon from the Pacific coast.

Fishing was traditionally the main industry in many parts of Atlantic Canada. It still is in some areas, with the provinces of Newfoundland and Labrador and Nova Scotia accounting for 80 percent of the region's catch. British Columbia's fishery, based mainly on salmon, is the country's largest. The federal government is responsible for the management of ocean fisheries and fisheries in national parks. The provincial governments manage freshwater fisheries within their boundaries.

MINING

Canada produces more than 60 different mineral products, making the mining industry a major factor in the country's economy.

In volume, Canada is one of the world's largest mineral exporters. It is the leading exporter of potash and uranium and ranks among the top five countries in the export of nickel, asbestos, gypsum, salt, molybelenum, titanium concentrate, aluminum, cadmium, cobalt, copper, gold, lead, silver, and platinum.

Canada exports about 80 percent of its mineral products to the United States, Japan, and the European Union. With the exception of a few minerals, Canada is able to meet its own domestic mineral needs.

The provincial governments are responsible for the exploration, development, conservation, and production of natural resources within their boundaries. To ensure a supply of metals and minerals, the mining industry continues to explore and map mineral deposits and other geological features, and develop new mining methods and equipment.

THE GOLD RUSH

In 1856 a gold prospector, James Huston, discovered a large amount of gold dust along the Fraser and Thompson rivers, which have their source in the Cariboo Mountains of British Columbia. When news of Fraser gold spread south, about 25,000 miners from the United States, Latin America, and Hawaii rushed north. At the height of the Fraser gold rush, about 10,000 miners were spread out over a 200-mile (320-km) area. Mining the Fraser was difficult. Melting snows engorged the river, and mining could not take place until August when the river was at its summer low. In winter the freezing cold and deep snows made mining dangerous and often impossible.

In 1862 an even bigger gold rush began when hopeful adventurers, following the Fraser north, hit the jackpot at William's Creek, in the Cariboo region. Many made a fortune—and squandered it just as quickly—but the real benefits of the Fraser and Cariboo gold rushes were the blossoming of the town of Victoria into a busy city and the opening up of the interior of British Columbia.

In 1896 gold was discovered in the Klondike by a prospector, George Washington Carmack, and his two companions, Skookum Jim and Tagish Charlie. The Klondike was Canada's greatest gold rush. It lasted a few spectacular years, from 1897 to 1900, during which $40 million in gold was mined in the area.

Conditions were harsh. The frozen ground had to be thawed out with wood fires before it could be excavated and the gold-bearing rock recovered. But that did not stop gold fever from infecting the thousands who flocked to the Klondike from all points of the globe. Dawson City grew into a boom town. At the height of the rush, the city had a population of about 30,000 people. Today, there are only about 2,000 residents.

ENERGY RESOURCES

Canada's energy is derived mostly from the burning of crude oil, natural gas, and coal, and from nuclear and river power. A small amount comes from solar and wind power and from biomass, which is plant or animal material such as grass, crops, or animal waste.

Canada is the world's third largest producer of natural gas and the eighth largest in total oil production. A large portion of the country's energy production is used up domestically. Nevertheless, Canada also manages to export energy, sending more than 80 percent of mined petroleum and natural gas and 5 to 10 percent of generated electricity south to the United States.

Canada's first oil reservoir that was worth extracting commercially was discovered in 1947 in Leduc, Alberta. By 2000 nearly 7 million oil wells had been drilled in the country. Canada has huge potential oil and gas reserves under the Arctic waters and the Atlantic Ocean off the eastern coast.

Canada also has abundant coal reserves. Mined as early as 1639, coal accounts for more than a tenth of Canada's energy supply needs. The provinces of Saskatchewan and Nova Scotia are almost completely dependent on coal for electricity. Canada exports coal to the Pacific Rim countries, Europe, and South America.

Wood is a popular source of energy in rural parts of Canada. Wood wastes and wood chips are also a source of fuel for heating.

Canada is the world's leading producer of hydroelectricity. There are major hydroelectricity projects in Newfoundland and Labrador, Ontario, Quebec, Manitoba, and British Columbia.

The Irving pulp mill in Saint John, New Brunswick.

TRADE

In 1988 Canada and the United States signed a free-trade agreement, which would serve as a mechanism to resolve trade disputes between the two countries in a fair and efficient manner. For individual travelers, the free-trade agreement reduced or eliminated customs duties on all goods of U.S. or Canadian origin purchased for personal use. Duties were lifted on consumer items such as computers, calculators, furniture, and clothing.

In 1992 Canada, the United States, and Mexico signed the North American Free Trade Agreement (NAFTA), creating the world's biggest and wealthiest free-trade market. Mexico is Canada's largest trade partner in Latin America. Under NAFTA, import duties that restrict trade and investment among the three countries will be gradually eliminated.

Vancouver harbor is a major point of exit for resource-rich British Columbia's export trade.

Canada has also committed itself to improving trade through trade organizations. It was an original member of the Asia-Pacific Economic Cooperation (APEC) group and joined the World Trade Organization (WTO) in 1995. Nevertheless, not all Canadians believe that NAFTA and trade organizations are beneficial to Canada. Opponents of the free-trade agreement fear that it will lead to job losses, business failures, and a flooding of the Canadian market with cheap-labor products. WTO and APEC meetings held in Canada have been met with protests organized by Canadians who feel that such groups harm local economies and that they aid only the rich and powerful.

THE CANADIAN WORKFORCE

In the late 1800s, almost half of all Canadian workers were farm workers. By 2002 the number of farm workers had dropped to 2 percent of the Canadian workforce, and only another 2 percent were employed in other primary industries.

The Canadian workforce is one of the most highly skilled and highly paid in the world. The average family income in 2001 was $79,980. Young Canadians entering the workforce prepare for jobs in fields that were unheard of just a few decades ago: advanced robotics, computer programming, agricultural engineering, and satellite communication.

Fifty-eight percent of the Canadian workforce works in the service sector, while trade and manufacturing respectively employ 16 and 15 percent of the workforce. Government workers form 5 percent of the workforce.

The flexible hours of part-time work and the lower cost of employee benefits it presents to companies have led to a rise in the number of part-time workers in Canada. More women are also joining the workforce. In 2002 they made up 46 percent of the workforce.

WORKING CONDITIONS

Canadian workers have come a long way since the days of a more farm-oriented economy but not without a struggle. Toward the end of the 19th century, the Royal Commission on the Relations of Labor and Capital in Canada revealed the hardships of the working class. People worked long

A woodcarver demonstrates his art near the Capilano Suspension Bridge in Vancouver, British Columbia.

CANADIAN TRADE UNIONS

The first Canadian unions were craft unions, uniting skilled workers such as printers, carpenters, painters, bakers, and tailors. But unions were considered illegal until 1872, when printers in Toronto campaigning for a nine-hour (instead of 10-hour) work day clashed with publishers. Following a mass protest in front of the legislative buildings in Toronto, the Canadian parliament passed the Trade Union Act, legalizing unions.

Another landmark in trade-union history occurred when workers realized they would have greater power if they formed a national organization. In 1886 the craft unions formed the Trades and Labor Congress of Canada (TLC). In 1902 the TLC joined the American Federation of Labor (AFL).

Other unions began to form rapidly. Unskilled workers not eligible to join the craft unions created industrial unions. In 1927 the various unions banded together to form the All-Canadian Congress of Labor (ACCL). In 1940 the ACCL linked up with the Congress of Industrial Organizations (CIO) in the United States and became the Canadian Congress of Labor (CCL).

Trouble accompanied the early years of Canadian union activity, especially in the years after World War II when strikes were frequent and often violent, and unions fought employers, the police, and the government. But out of the turmoil came cohesion. Craft unions and industrial unions, together with several other national unions, joined in 1956 to form the Canadian Labor Congress (CLC). Today, the CLC represents more than 2.5 million workers in Canada and works with other activist groups to protect and promote workers' rights.

hours, children also worked, wages were low, and money could be deducted as a fine for perceived misconduct.

Today, Canadian workers are protected by labor laws. The Canadian Labor Code regulates federal jobs and provides a standard by which workers in Canada can measure how they are being treated by their employers. Among other things, the code limits hours on the job to a maximum of eight hours a day or 40 hours a week. Generally, no more than eight hours of overtime work a week is allowed, and overtime pay must be at least one and a half times the regular rate. Minimum wages are frequently reviewed and adjusted according to the state of the economy and the effects of inflation. Employers must give employees at least two weeks paid vacation every year.

In addition, a human rights code prohibits job discrimination on the basis of race, religion, national origin, color, gender, sexual orientation, age, or marital status.

ENVIRONMENT

CANADA HAS A WIDE RANGE of ecosystems and natural-resource industries to match. The country faces some difficult environmental challenges. Fortunately, Canadians and their government have realized their responsibility toward future generations in caring for the environment.

Ecotourism is a growing sector of the Canadian economy. Some of the ecotourism projects have been initiated by the indigenous peoples with aid from the federal government. They have gradually come to see ecotourism as a way of ensuring their communities' economic development as well as of encouraging a greater appreciation for nature among Canadians and visitors.

Above: **Excited whale-watching tourists in Tadoussac, Quebec.**

Opposite: **Set amid the lush forest of the Capilano River Regional Park in Vancouver, British Columbia, the suspension bridge is popular with tourists.**

ECOLOGICAL ZONES

An ecological zone is an area where organisms survive as a system with their surroundings. It is defined by, among other factors, its climate, landforms, water features, and vegetation, and the presence of human activities such as agriculture and recreation.

Canada has 15 terrestrial and five marine ecological zones. It shares some of its ecological zones with the United States. Canada's terrestrial ecological zones are the Arctic Cordillera, the Northern Arctic, the Southern Arctic, the Taiga Plains, the Taiga Shield, the Taiga Cordillera, the Atlantic Maritime, the Mixedwood Plains, the Boreal Shield, the Boreal Plains, the Boreal Cordillera, the Prairies, the Pacific Maritime, the Montane Cordillera, and the Hudson Plains. Its marine zones are the Pacific Marine, the Arctic Archipelago Marine, the Northwest Atlantic Marine, the Atlantic Marine, and the Arctic Basin Marine.

THE TREES

Canada's first national park, the magnificent and renowned Banff, was created in 1885 to preserve the beauty of the Rocky Mountains. Today, there are 39 national parks and more than 3,000 provincial protected areas. The national parks, which cover slightly more than 2 percent of the nation's land, are managed by the federal government. The provincial governments manage the provincial parks.

While Canada is 33rd in the world in the percentage of land that lies in protected areas, it is among the top in total protected area. In 2001 roughly 7.3 percent of Canada's total land area was protected. The provinces of British Columbia and Alberta account for the largest portion (12.5 percent) of the nation's total protected land area.

Responsible forestry has developed with the parks system. The history of Canadian forestry has many examples of wasteful logging based on the erroneous belief that the forests were an inexhaustible resource.

It became increasingly obvious in the 20th century that forests were in fact exhaustible and that more responsible forestry practices were needed. In 1906 Canada's first forestry program was introduced at the University of Toronto.

POLLUTION

As global warming threatens much of Canada's economy, pollution, especially from greenhouse gas emissions, has become a major issue. In the first few years of the 21st century, Canada suffered an increase in drought due to global warming, and the consequent loss of billions of dollars in agricultural revenue. Unusually mild winters stimulated the mountain pine beetle infestation in pine forests, while hot and dry summers led to record numbers of forest fires, especially in British Columbia. Global warming has also affected Canada's fish stocks, while pollution-related illnesses have raised health-care costs.

Acid rain is another threat to Canada's natural beauty. The burning of coal in power plants, the smelting of nickel and copper, and the use of motor vehicles produce harmful gases, such as nitrous and sulfurous oxides, which combine with water vapor in the atmosphere and fall as acid rain. Acid rain pollutes rivers and lakes and damages plant, animal, and human life.

Above: **Thick smoke from a lumberyard's furnace pollutes the air around Crownest Pass, Alberta.**

Opposite: **The Sunwapta Falls in Jasper National Park, Alberta, is a stunning example of Canada's excellent national parks system.**

Since 1980 Canada has reduced its acid rain-causing emissions by more than half.

DEALING WITH POLLUTION   Canada holds national environmental events, such as Environment Week and Clean Air Day, to promote environmental awareness. Carpool programs give special highway lanes in cities to vehicles with multiple occupants, and more energy-efficient homes have been built. People generally realize their environmental responsibility and try to do their bit to protect the environment. For example, an increasing number of drivers are choosing to commute by bicycle rather than by car.

Canada also participates in the Kyoto Protocol, an international agreement to lower greenhouse gas emissions.

ALTERNATIVE SOURCES OF ENERGY

Energy generation is one of the largest contributors to air pollution in Canada. In 2000 some 36 percent of Canada's greenhouse-gas emissions came from the power and petroleum industries, while transportation accounted for another 25 percent. Relief is in sight, as natural gas, the cleanest fossil fuel, replaces coal and petroleum and the use of renewable energy sources becomes more efficient.

Hydropower is a major renewable source, particularly in British Columbia and Ontario. Hydropower is nearly pollution-free, but its production requires the damming of rivers. Dams disrupt river flow and cause surrounding areas to flood. This displaces local wildlife and can disturb the ecological balance of the area. To minimize the impact of dams, the Canadian government has developed smaller hydropower plants, especially in more remote regions.

Nuclear power is also controversial. There are 22 nuclear plants in Ontario, Quebec, and New Brunswick. While nuclear sources do not produce greenhouse gases, they do produce radioactive waste, which is far worse in many ways. In Canada, it looks like nuclear power is on its way out. Many of the nation's nuclear plants have had serious safety and productivity problems. They may finally be shut down rather than repaired at enormous cost.

Wind power is the latest trend in renewable energy. With the abundance of wind in many provinces, wind power may become the most viable form of clean energy for Canada. Another promising source is biomass, mostly organic waste from which methane gas is derived. The potential of solar power is hampered by the abundance of clouds in coastal regions and by overcast winter days throughout much of the country for parts of the year.

In the south of Alberta, wind-turbine farms are becoming as commonplace as cattle farms.

SOMETHING DIFFERENT UNDER THE HOOD?

Canada is a world leader in cutting-edge low- and zero-emission automotive technologies. Westport, a company in Vancouver, British Columbia, produces diesel-engine variants that run on propane or natural gas, mostly for heavy trucks and buses. These engines, being developed with Cummins, the world's largest diesel-engine manufacturer, are capable of reducing harmful emissions by up to 60 percent compared to traditional diesel engines. The "clean" engines have attracted significant world attention. They could play a major role in helping countries reach pollution-reduction levels agreed on in the Kyoto Protocol.

The new technology is of particular interest because it is off the drawing board and entering production. Ballard Power Systems, based in Burnaby, British Columbia, is probably the best-known company producing fuel-cell technology. Fuel cells burn hydrogen and produce large amounts of power with water as the only by-product.

While not likely to be widely available for some time, the fuel cell may be the power source of the future for everything from buses and cars to laptop computers to electricity generators. It is efficient and clean, and runs on the most common element on the planet. Though the concept has been around since 1839, the technology is only now becoming practical.

RECYCLING

Recycling is another way in which Canadians try to take care of their environment. The concept of "reduce, reuse, and recycle" has become increasingly commonplace in the country, especially since the last few years of the 20th century.

All Canadian cities, and most of the smaller towns, have recycling centers where used bottles, paper, plastics, metals, and other materials can be deposited. Refundable deposits on packaged drink sales have so effectively encouraged recycling that drink containers are now rarely seen on the ground or in the trash. The recycling of hazardous materials such as transmission fluid and motor oil has also been strongly promoted, and the proportion of oil recycled grew from 20 percent in 1990 to 70 percent in 2001.

Environmental consciousness costs, but Canadians understand that it is necessary. For example, a homeowner who buys a can of paint pays a small recycling fee in addition to the cost of the paint. The Canadian government is also working with the electronics industry to implement recycling programs for old equipment such as stereos and computers.

CLEAN, FRESH WATER

While Canada contains roughly one-quarter of the world's fresh water supply, only 7 percent of that is renewable (non-ocean draining). This water supply is threatened by acid rain and waste, and vast amounts of water are wasted through pipe leaks and inefficient toilets and shower heads—problems the United States also faces.

Canada and the United States comanage the Great Lakes and have a mutual interest in water conservation. Canada's municipal governments have developed water-conservation programs to encourage residents to save water. Such programs have been quite successful in educating Canadians on the importance of protecting their water supply.

Canada's towns, such as Salmon Arm in British Columbia, are stepping up efforts to conserve water and keep it clean.

CANADIANS

THE EARLY STORY OF CANADA is one of its people—the original inhabitants of the land, the colonizers from Europe, and the immigrants who came from afar seeking a better future—and the challenges they faced. For the indigenous peoples, the challenge was first to learn to survive off the land. Later it became a struggle to maintain and preserve their ways of life. For the colonizers and immigrants, the challenge was to learn to adapt to the new and often hostile land.

ROOM TO BREATHE

Canada is the world's second-largest country in land area, and one of the richest. Despite a history of immigration, it is one of the most thinly populated countries in the world, ranked 35th by population size. The 31.6 million people living in Canada are not evenly distributed across the 10 provinces and three territories.

Much of the north remains largely uninhabited. Around 85 percent of Canadians live within 186 miles (300 km) of Canada's southern border, with 62 percent concentrated in Ontario and Quebec, near the Great Lakes and the Saint Lawrence River. Large parts of Nova Scotia, New Brunswick, and the Gaspé Peninsula in eastern Quebec are thinly populated.

Opposite: **Inuit girls at a playground on Baffin Island.**

Below: **Two boys in Sydney, Nova Scotia.**

Chinatown in Vancouver. An example of Canada's cosmopolitan make-up.

THEY CAME, THEY SAW, THEY STAYED

Immigration has played an important part in the history of Canada. At the time of Confederation, the descendants of European immigrants, United Empire Loyalists, and First Peoples made up the population.

The English and the French were followed by Scottish, German, and Swiss immigrants who settled in Nova Scotia. During the American Revolution (1775–83), about 50,000 United Loyalists left America and settled in the Atlantic provinces and Ontario to avoid being part of the new American republic. The great potato famine in Ireland in the mid-19th century brought tens of thousands of Irish settlers.

The late 19th century also saw the first wave of Ukrainian immigrants. They were fleeing from the extreme poverty, overpopulation, and discriminatory policies of their homeland, which was under the Austrian monarchy. Most of them settled in the prairie provinces.

Asians were also an integral part of the early history of immigration in Canada. Poverty was usually the reason why many Chinese, Japanese, Pakistanis, and East Indians left their homelands. Many of the Japanese who settled in Canada during the early times also emigrated to escape serving in the Japanese army when military conscription was introduced in Japan in 1873.

At the start of the 20th century, the Canadian government began the big push to populate the huge, empty prairie lands. Through a massive publicity campaign, Europeans, then beset by poverty, overcrowding, persecution, and other troubles, were lured across the sea by the promise of free land—all they had to do was clear it, farm it, and make it their home. From 1910 to 1914, about 3 million settlers flooded into Canada.

A SAFE HAVEN

Since World War II, Canada has experienced another period of population growth that was first fueled by a "baby boom" and then by immigration.

Tens of thousands of immigrants from eastern and southern Europe were admitted. In addition, Canada took in many Ugandan, Chilean, Czechoslovakian, Hungarian, and Southeast Asian refugees. By the 1970s, the country had become known as a land of opportunity, and a magnet for people around the world seeking a better life. That created a trend that has persisted to this day. People facing an uncertain or troubled future in their home countries continue to look to Canada as a safe haven.

In 2002 a new Immigration and Refugee Protection Act was adopted. The state of the country's population, economy, society, and culture are all taken into consideration when determining policy, while the aim is to help families reunite. The act does not discriminate on racial or ethnic grounds, and recognizes Canada's obligation as one of the world's most favored countries for refugees.

Canada is a multicultural society where all creeds and colors are accepted.

FIRST PEOPLES TODAY

An Inuit woman involved in the traditional activity of hide preparation.

It has often been said that there are two founding peoples in Canada —the French and the British. But a different view is becoming more prominent—that the land the French and the British claimed to have discovered had already been "founded" by the people who were there thousands of years before.

Anthropologists estimate that Canada had an indigenous population of about 350,000 when the Europeans arrived. In the following decades, this population declined because of disease, starvation, and warfare, threatening the existence of their unique cultures. At the time of Confederation, there were between 100,000 and 125,000 First Nations peoples in Canada.

The downward trend has reversed, and today the Aboriginal population is growing at a faster rate than the rest of the population. In 2001 more than 1 million Canadians reported having aboriginal ancestry. Inuit make up less than 10 percent of the indigenous population.

As a result of treaties, most of Canada's First Nations peoples live in communities called "Indian bands" on reserves set aside for their exclusive use. But the reserves are not as rich in resources as was their ancestors' land.

There are 614 bands living in 2,720 reserves. The bands vary in size, the largest being the Six

Nations of the Grand River in Ontario, which has about 21,618 members. Socially and economically, the Aboriginals are generally poorer than other Canadians due to the discrimination they faced in the early years. But their situation is improving. Close to half of all First Nations peoples in reserves depend on social assistance from the government.

The unemployment rate among the indigenous population is more than three times that of the national population. But one must remember that the number of unemployed includes many people who continue their traditional forms of work, such as hunting and fishing, which earn them just enough to live on.

With improving conditions, the First Nations peoples are slowly making the government and other Canadians aware that they were once free, self-sustaining peoples. Today, aboriginal councils manage almost all aboriginal affairs. More indigenous children are attending school, some operated by the bands, some by the government. Aboriginal Business Canada, a government agency, has provided financial and other support to around 5,000 aboriginal businesses.

The indigenous peoples are seeking their own forms of self-government. With the creation of Nunavut, they have begun to achieve that goal, which they hope will enable them to assume their proper place in Canadian society while maintaining the rich diversity of their traditional cultures that evolved over thousands of years before European contact.

An indigenous girl in traditional dress.

NOT ALL WERE EQUAL

Not everyone who came to Canada in the 19th century received an open-arms welcome from Canadians, who were then mostly of English heritage. The policies of the Canadian government at that time favored English, Scottish, and American immigrants, who were believed to fit best into Canada's established community. But people from other countries kept coming in the belief that they could have a better life in Canada.

Many of the early immigrants gravitated to the cities rather than remain in the isolated countryside. They provided the labor needed in mines, lumberyards, and factories, and they worked on the railway, cleared land, and helped build settlements.

But many Canadians did not take kindly to their presence, vital though it was. Racist immigration laws were passed and enforced. They included several anti-Chinese laws, which first imposed a "head tax" of $40 (this was finally raised to $400) on every Chinese entering the country, and culminated

in the Chinese Immigration Act of 1923, prohibiting any more Chinese from entering Canada. It took 24 years for the act to be repealed. Chinese immigrants who were already in Canada were denied citizenship rights and the right to vote.

During World War II, Japanese immigrants living within a 100-mile (160-km) band along the Pacific coast were taken inland because their loyalty to Canada was suspect.

Now things are very different. Canadians have embraced the principles of diversity and multiculturalism. Mindful of their checkered past, they have enshrined within their society a broad framework of laws and policies such as the Charter of Rights and Freedoms, the Human Rights Act, and the Multiculturalism Act. These ensure that all individuals, regardless of where they come from, have a right to equal opportunities within Canadian society.

Members of the Kingston German Society in Ontario gather in traditional dress to celebrate their heritage.

MULTICULTURALISM

While the United States is thought of as a melting pot, in which many different ethnic and cultural ingredients blend to create a new society, Canada is often called a mosaic—the sum rather than product of all the different ethnic and cultural groups, with each group still retaining its distinctive characteristics.

Multiculturalism is the policy that has arisen from this mosaic. It is Canada's policy "to recognize all Canadians as full and equal participants in Canadian society." The federal Department of State and the provincial departments of Citizenship and Social Services issue publications and have many services designed to help newcomers integrate into the country.

PREFERRED IMMIGRANTS

In the 19th and early 20th centuries, when the government was actively recruiting prospective immigrants, it had a scale of preferences. British and American settlers were "preferred," followed by French, Belgians, Dutch, Scandinavians, and Germans. Italians, Slavs, and Greeks were less desirable, followed by Asians and Africans. Today, Canada makes no such preferences and is one of the world's most racially tolerant and multicultural countries.

THE ELUSIVE CANADIAN

In a large country consisting of immigrants from many lands, it is not easy to pin down the Canadian identity. The problem seems to have provoked an endless discussion among Canadians on the question "Who are we?" But it is a discussion done with typical Canadian humor, self-deprecating and good-natured.

Attitudes are now changing. Canadians have become more comfortable with themselves. Where Canadians were once restrained in showing their emotions, they are now less ambivalent about displaying their pride for their country. Canadians have always been proud of their country, but it is traditionally a quiet form of patriotism that bubbles to the surface only on occasions such as winning the hockey gold at the Winter Olympics.

Canadians see themselves as peaceful people with little interest in wars and conflict and running other peoples' lives. If Canadians should get involved in disputes, they are very likely to consult all parties involved and work on getting a compromise that benefits all. Canadians, in fact, pride themselves as mediators.

Perhaps the reason for the pacifist attitude of Canadians is a history that is remarkably free of bloodshed, war, or revolution, which often mark the birth of a nation. Canada outgrew its dependence on Britain in a slow and hesitant manner. In fact, Canada

Many Canadians are relaxed and easy-going.

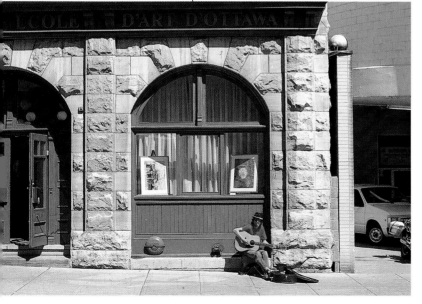

never completely severed ties with Britain and still has a close relationship with its former colonizer. There is a general view that it took almost a century after Confederation for Canadians to come to recognize themselves as Canadians.

But Canadians' pride for their country extends beyond sports and diplomacy. They love their wide open land and its resources, and they greatly appreciate the freedoms that their constitution has given them: to vote, to practice one's religion, to work or go to school regardless of one's ethnic heritage or gender, to speak one's own language, to voice one's personal opinion.

Canadians are finally coming to accept themselves for who they are —a peace-loving united group of people with diverse backgrounds and ways of seeing the world.

ON CANADIANS AND THEIR IDENTITY

"I know the worth of this unprecedented idea, the idea of unity without uniformity which is the distinctive mark of Canada, the stamp of Canadian identity."—Duff Roblin, premier of Manitoba (1958–67).

"I think our identity will have to be something which is partly British, partly French, partly American, partly derived from a variety of other influences which are too numerous even to catalogue."—former senator Eugene Forsey (1904–91).

"Dull and introverted and all the rest of it though we may be, Canadians have as a people a national gift for tolerance and an acquired skill at compromise."—Richard Gwyn, newspaper columnist.

"I think being Canadian is just acknowledging the fact that we live in such a great country…It's feeling a weird sense of pride when we win gold at the Olympics, even if you hate sports. It's realizing that we are…ONE country, united and multicultural."—Ashleigh Viveiros, student.

"Canadians are…understated. To understand the identity that exists in our hearts think of our sweeping majestic home, its quiet serene beauty."—Debora O'Neil.

LIFESTYLE

THE FAMILY INSTITUTION is alive and well in Canada. In 1996, 85 percent of Canadian families were two-parent households. However, the pressures of modern living have changed the structure and demographic composition of the family.

With a longer life expectancy, the population is aging, and there are more elderly people at home. At the same time, improved transportation has made travel from one part of the country to another quick and easy, and many young Canadians move out of their family homes to live and work in other towns or provinces.

FAMILY LIFE

The size of the average Canadian family is getting smaller. People are marrying later in life and having fewer children than their parents did. There is also an increasing tendency for young, single members of the family to leave home and set up their lives and careers away from their hometowns. Other factors that have contributed to the shrinking of the Canadian family include an increasing number of single-parent families and of unmarried women choosing to have children and raise them on their own.

Since World War II, more and more couples in Canada have been entering into relationships and forming families without actually getting married. Such family arrangements, known as common-law unions, are found especially among younger or divorced Canadians. Nevertheless, many common-law unions eventually end in marriage.

Since 1968, when divorce laws were relaxed in Canada, divorce has been on the rise. Since the mid-1980s, almost half of all marriages in the country have ended in divorce. High divorce rates may be one of the reasons why young Canadians are reluctant to marry.

"Yes, Alec, it is I, your father, speaking." And with these words, the first message was transmitted by long-distance telephone from Melville Bell who was in Brantford, Ontario, to his son, Alexander Graham Bell, 8 miles (13 km) away in Paris, Ontario, in 1876. Since then, Canadians have not stopped talking on the telephone.

Opposite: **Urban Canadians enjoy their leisure time at sidewalk cafés along Victoria Row in Charlottetown, Prince Edward Island.**

Preschool children on an outing to Toronto's city hall.

GROWING UP IN CANADA

In many Canadian families, both parents work. Many Canadian children have thus experienced being in the care of someone other than their parents. The caregiver may be another child's parent, who may look after several children at home during office hours, a teacher at a daycare center, or a baby-sitter.

Most children start school by age 5 or 6. By Canadian law, children must attend school from ages 6 through 16. School usually begins with kindergarten and finishes in either 11th or 12th grade. Generally, elementary school runs from kindergarten to sixth grade, junior high school covers the years from seventh to eighth or ninth grade, and senior high school starts in ninth or 10th grade and ends in 11th or 12th grade.

After graduation, students find a job or continue formal education at community colleges, technical institutes, or universities. The University of Toronto, University of British Columbia, and McGill University in Montreal are three of many well-known and internationally acclaimed Canadian universities.

Canadian children learn to be independent at an early age. Boys and girls learn to socialize with the opposite sex from the time they are very young, because most Canadian schools are coeducational. How to be attractive and popular in school, dating, and going steady are concerns that come early in the lives of Canadian adolescents, and sex education is part of the school curriculum. Students are also taught about the dangerous effects of drugs and alcohol abuse.

Many young Canadians are introduced to working life while still in school. It is not uncommon for Canadian students to do occasional odd jobs, such as raking leaves, washing cars, or mowing lawns, or to take on a part-time job, such as having a paper route.

Canadians leave home almost immediately after graduation from school, either to go to college or a university or to enter the workforce. Either way, their pursuits during their late teenage years may take them away from their hometown.

DEFINING MARRIAGE FOR CANADA'S YOUTH

Debate is raging in Canada on a major 21st-century issue—do same-sex couples have the right to marry legally? This debate and resulting laws will greatly influence young Canadians' ideas of marriage and family.

A poll carried out in 2003 suggested that Canadians were evenly split on the matter of allowing same-sex couples to marry and register their marriage. The provinces are also divided—Quebec, Ontario, British Columbia, Nova Scotia, and Manitoba supported same-sex rights, while Alberta, Prince Edward Island, and New Brunswick opposed.

Numerous court decisions, particularly in Ontario and Quebec, have opposed existing laws as being disciminatory toward same-sex couples when it comes to benefits and rights given to couples in civil unions. However, the definition of marriage as a union between a man and a woman still holds. In 2000 the parliament passed Bill C-23, giving same-sex couples equality for common-law benefits. In 2002 both the Ontario and Quebec courts declared current marriage laws discriminatory.

The current government has asked the Supreme Court of Canada to decide if same-sex marriage is constitutional. The Supreme Court will give its decision sometime end-2004. Same-sex unions have received support from the Netherlands, New Zealand, a few U.S. states, and the European parliament. It remains to be seen how Canada will resolve the issue.

GROWING OLD IN CANADA

Canada has one of the highest life expectancies in the world. Canadian women can expect to live for almost 83 years, while Canadian men can expect to live for about 76 years. This, coupled with the fact that people are waiting longer to have children and then choosing to have fewer children than the generation before them, has resulted in a population with a greater proportion of older people.

The elderly population is growing more rapidly than any other age group in the country. When Canadians retire, life is far from over; often

Boating with the grand-children. Whatever their age, Canadians love the outdoors.

it just takes a new turn. Free from the need to earn a living, retirees find other pursuits to occupy their time. They join choirs, form musical or theatrical groups, go hiking, take up new hobbies, or even go back to school. Many volunteer their skills and services in Canada or abroad. The elderly also find love during their golden years. Marriages between Canadians age 65 or older are common.

The importance of the older segment of Canadian society is reflected in the country's social infrastructure and facilities, which cater to the needs of the elderly. Businesses also recognize that they can make a lot of money from Canada's senior citizens, who thus enjoy discount days in stores, lower fees for services, and cheaper travel.

Centers for senior citizens have been developed in every province. These are multipurpose centers that provide community social services to elderly citizens. They offer all kinds of recreational, cultural, and educational activities. Housing developers also build apartments and condominiums that are rented or sold exclusively to older Canadians.

A WELFARE STATE

Canada is a welfare state, which means the government provides many social services to the public. Health and social programs, such as Medicare, Canada Pension Plan, Canada Assistance Plan, and a Guaranteed Income Supplement ensure that Canadians will be cared for in the event they become disabled, unemployed, or otherwise unable to provide for themselves.

This couple can expect to be cared for the whole of their lives under Canada's welfare system.

Depending on the kind of government that comes to power, whether liberal or socialist in outlook, these social programs may either be cut back to reduce the financial burden they place on the government or increased to be compatible with the social philosophy of reducing inequality in society. Low-income families with children under age 18 receive monthly payments, called child tax benefits, from the government to help with the financial cost of raising their children.

Canada's nationwide health insurance system is designed to ensure that everyone in the country receives medical care and treatment when they require it so that no one is denied access because they are too poor to afford it. The provinces and territories organize and finance their own health insurance plans; the federal government contributes to it. People pay toward the plan, but the amount they pay varies according to their income level. Patients are not charged directly when they visit a doctor or are hospitalized.

Both employers and employees make contributions to the Canada Pension Plan, which then provides a pension to workers and their families when they retire. Employment Insurance is a nationwide program that helps people who are out of work.

WOMEN IN CANADA

The organized women's movement in Canada developed in the late 19th century, focusing mainly on gaining voting rights for women, access for women to higher education, and equality in the work place.

In the late 1970s, women's organizations brought cases of wife and child abuse to the attention of the public. This led to a law that permits intervention in cases of domestic assault. Women were also successful in getting the principle of sexual equality incorporated in the Charter of Rights and Freedoms that formed part of the 1982 Canadian Constitution.

Women make up an increasing proportion of Canada's workforce (nearly 47 percent in 2003). The majority of married women have a paying job outside the home, and the number of self-employed women rose from 433,800 in 1982 to 820,700 in 2002.

Despite the advances that have been made with regard to the status of women in society, the fact still remains that the majority of Canadian women generally hold two jobs—one in the workforce and one at home. Also, though women may have caught up with men in terms of numbers, they still have some way to go in wage parity. In 2001 women earned on average 36 percent less than men in Canada.

Women are aware of their right to independence and to control their own lives. They join unions and other organizations that aim to establish equal pay for equal work, maternity leave and benefits, adequate daycare facilities, the end of discrimination in the workplace, and protection against sexual harassment.

Canadian women have gained equality in many respects and continue to raise societal consciousness of women's rights.

MILESTONES FOR CANADIAN WOMEN

In 1867 Emily Jennings Stowe became the first Canadian woman with a medical degree to practice medicine in Canada. Emily was rejected as a student by the University of Toronto because she was a woman. She earned her degree in the United States and later campaigned for the admission of women to Canadian universities. In 1883 Stowe's daughter, Augusta, became the first woman to earn a medical degree in Canada. She studied at the Toronto School of Medicine.

In 1872 married women in Ontario were allowed to own property. British Columbia passed a similar law later that year.

In 1897 Clara Brett Martin became the first woman lawyer in Canada and the British Empire.

In 1916, after a long campaign, women in Manitoba, Alberta, and Saskatchewan won the right to vote. Women in Ontario and British Columbia were allowed to vote the following year.

In 1921 Agnes MacPhail became the first woman Member of Parliament.

In 1951 Charlotte Whitton became mayor of Ottawa, the first woman to become mayor of a large city.

In 1960 the Canadian Bill of Rights was passed forbidding any gender-based discrimination.

In 1971 the Canada Labor Code was amended to provide women with a maternity leave of 17 weeks. The code also prohibits discrimination in the workplace on the grounds of marital status or gender.

In 1980 Jeanne Sauvé became the first woman Speaker of the House of Commons.

In 1983 Roberta Bondar became the first Canadian woman to become an astronaut. She was one of six scientists chosen as Canada's original astronauts.

In 1984 Jeanne Sauvé became the first woman to be appointed governor-general.

In 1985, thanks to the determined efforts of indigenous women such as Jeannette Vivian Corbiere Lavell, the Indian Act was amended to restore to indigenous women their indigenous rights, which according to previous laws they lost by marrying non-indigenous Canadians.

In 1989 Audrey McLaughlin became the first woman to lead a major North American political party, the New Democratic Party.

In 1991 Rita Johnston became the premier of British Columbia and the first woman premier in Canada.

In 1993 Kim Campbell became Canada's first woman prime minister.

The hustle and bustle of Toronto, Canada's largest city.

PEOPLE ON THE MOVE

Canada is so large that since its earliest days the method of getting from one place to another has been an important aspect of life. The country owes its unity to the railway, which overcame muskeg (bogs), swamps, and mountain ranges to link the Pacific and Atlantic coasts.

Canada has two major railways: the Canadian Pacific Railway and the Canadian National Railway. There are also several smaller local ones.

Passenger rail service is provided by a government company called VIA Rail, but people usually drive, use intercity bus services, or travel by air over long distances. As a result, VIA Rail cut back on its services, though lately this trend has begun to reverse. A mainstay of VIA Rail is its popular Western Transcontinental service from Vancouver across the Rocky Mountains to Edmonton, Winnipeg, and Toronto.

Major international airports link Canada with the rest of the world. There are also many large and small airports throughout the country that cater to domestic travel. Canada's main international airline is Air Canada. Other smaller air carriers offer air links with most of the communities across the country. They are especially important to the small, remote communities in the north that get most of their services by air.

Most important is the network of roads that crisscross Canada. Roads of all kinds ensure that people and goods can travel to almost every part of the country. The Trans-Canada Highway, which is 4,725 miles (7,604

THE ALASKA HIGHWAY

Canada's first roads were built for military purposes. A prime example was the Alaska Highway, nicknamed the Alcan Highway. The Japanese attack on Pearl Harbor in 1941 made the U.S. government realize the vulnerability of Alaska's shipping lanes to an attack. An inland route to Alaska was thus deemed a military necessity.

In exchange for the right-of-way through Canada, the U.S. government paid for the construction of the highway. For eight months in 1942, 11,000 American soldiers and thousands more Canadian and American civilians worked on the highway from both north and south. In 1946 the Canadian portion of the highway was turned over to the Canadian government.

The Alaska Highway stretches 1,488 miles (2,395 km) from Dawson Creek, British Columbia, to Delta Junction near Fairbanks, Alaska.

km) long and took more than half a century to complete, stretches from St. John's, Newfoundland and Labrador, to Victoria, British Columbia. Intercity buses provide an even more important link between cities than either air or rail. The three largest bus companies in Canada are Greyhound, Voyageur, and Gray Line. They allow Canadians to travel anywhere from the Pacific to the Atlantic and down into the United States. In 2002 there were more than 12 million passenger cars in Canada. Cars are necessary for work, shopping, and recreation. Many families own more than one vehicle.

Even when they are not on the move, Canadians cover the miles by telephone. The use of the telephone began with its invention in 1876 by Alexander Graham Bell, an American who resided in Canada. Almost every home in Canada has a telephone, often with more than one extension. Cell phones, answering machines, and facsimile machines are part and parcel of being connected in Canada. As of 2000, more than half of Canadians used the Internet, with usage among teenagers being the greatest at 90 percent.

Waiting for the bus. Buses are one of the many ways by which Canadians get around in their cities.

COUNTRY MOUSE AND CITY MOUSE

Since the 19th century, Canadians have been gravitating toward urban centers. Nearly 80 percent of Canadians live in an urban environment. The percentage of urban population varies from province to province. In Ontario, British Columbia, and Alberta, most of the population is urban, while in other parts of Canada, such as in the Atlantic provinces, many people still live in small towns and villages. In Prince Edward Island, the majority of the population is still rural.

Canada's cities, like cities elsewhere, have a central downtown area dominated by business activities. Around this core are residential communities with their own infrastructure of shopping centers, businesses, and services.

Life in the big city is exciting, and entertainment is available day and night. But the bustle of urban living and the crowds bring problems of violence, racial tension, pollution, and stress. Nevertheless, while urbanization generally leads to more crime, Canada's crime rate has fallen over the last decade.

Relaxing and having a drink in Vancouver, British Columbia.

Many small towns are dominated by one industry that acts as the major employer. There are logging towns, mining towns, and fishing villages. They range from small settlements of a hundred or so residents to towns and villages of a few thousand. Some small settlements are so remote that their only link with the rest of the country is by chartered planes.

CARING FOR THE ENVIRONMENT

Canadians, like so many other people in developed countries, are great consumers. At the local garbage dump, paper products—newspapers, packaging, telephone books, mail-order catalogues, and advertising flyers—make up about half the volume of trash. Plastics, in the form of packaging, bottles, appliances, construction materials, and so on, make up about a quarter of the garbage.

Canadians produce about 1,474 pounds (670 kg) of residential waste per person per year. Add to that pollution caused by industrial waste and a lifestyle in which two cars per family is the norm, and the impression one may get is that Canadians are a wasteful people.

That perception is becoming less true, as more Canadians understand the importance of caring for the environment—for their own sake and for the sake of future generations. Features in newspapers, magazines, and on television increasingly focus on the effects of pollution, highlighting disappearing forests and wildlife and what people can do to help. Government programs and increased public awareness are helping to reduce pollution and waste throughout Canada.

Municipalities and environmental groups encourage people to reduce the amount of garbage by reusing anything that they can and recycling what they cannot. Recyclable items, such as plastics, newspapers, metal cans, and cardboard, are brought to collection centers, sorted, and sold to manufacturers who turn them into new products. Big stores and supermarkets collect used plastic and paper shopping bags for recycling.

Though pollution is not uncommon in Canada, Canadians are becoming more and more environmentally conscious.

RELIGION

CANADA'S HISTORY is inextricably bound with religion. The indigenous peoples were filled with the spirit of the land and a reverence for nature and creation. When the French explorers came, they brought with them missionaries who introduced Christianity to the indigenous peoples.

In later years, Canada became a refuge for people suffering from religious persecution in their homelands. They went to Canada, where they could practice their own faiths in peace.

The millions who followed in the footsteps of the early immigrants to Canada introduced even more diversity into the religious fabric of the country. The freedom to practice one's own religion is entrenched in and protected by the Charter of Rights and Freedoms.

INDIGENOUS BELIEFS

The first peoples of Canada consist of many communities, but all of them have in common a deep spiritual relationship with the land and nature. They see themselves as a part of a world of interrelated spiritual forms. They revere the animals, the trees, and the land.

When people hunted animals for food, they treated the animal with great respect. A hunter would talk or sing to a bear before killing it, assuring the animal that its death was necessary only because he and his family needed it for food. A tree would not be cut down to build a canoe until its spirit was first appeased.

Myths were very important to the indigenous peoples. They told the story of creation and the origin of the moon, the sun, and the stars. They explained the meaning of various religious rituals. Visions and dreams had a lot of significance. Young Huron would seek a vision of their guardian spirit, who would reveal to them their personal chants, which they were to sing when in danger.

Opposite: **The colorful interior of the Cathedral Basilica of Notre Dame in Montreal, Quebec.**

Below: **An Inuit funeral mask. The Inuit believe that specters and ghosts haunt the world.**

Statues of Canada's original church fathers keep watch over Quebec City.

HEALING RITUALS Many indigenous communities in Canada had an elite group of shamans, or medicine men, who were spiritually powerful and could heal the sick. The Ojibway underwent a purification ritual, entering a sweat lodge where the scented vapors of an intensely hot, herbal sauna cleansed their bodies and spirits.

The Huron and Iroquois peoples had curing societies. The Iroquois False Face Curing Society used carved wooden masks that they believed possessed a spiritual force that gave special curative powers to wearers of the masks. Transformation masks, used by the Pacific Coast peoples, were worn during religious ceremonies to show their belief in the interconnectedness of people and animals. The masks opened and closed to reveal either a human or an animal face as the wearer pulled the strings.

CONVERTING THE FIRST PEOPLES

When the French and the English reached the shores of North America, they perceived the indigenous peoples as savages and heathens and believed that it was their task to bring enlightenment to them. Jacques Cartier introduced Christianity to Canada in 1534 when he landed on

THE POTLATCH CEREMONY

The potlatch ceremony was a common practice of the Pacific Coast communities in which a chief invited people to a celebration of feasting, dancing, and gift-giving. Potlatches were held to mark rites of initiation, to mourn the dead, or to celebrate the investiture of a new chief.

At the potlatch, which could last for days, the host chief presented gifts to his guests. The value of the gift corresponded directly to the guest's social ranking. The greater the prestige of the chief, the more wealth he distributed in gifts. When his guests held their own potlatches, they were expected to give even more lavishly or they would be shamed. A chief who made himself poor by giving lavishly at a potlatch ceremony could count on having his wealth returned at subsequent potlatch ceremonies where he would be a guest.

The potlatch ceremony was therefore important in establishing the status, rank, and privileges of the indigenous peoples. However, it was not understood as being an important ritual by the federal government and was banned. The ban was lifted in 1951, and potlatches are being held again today but never on the same scale as in the past.

the Gaspé Peninsula and planted a great cross. Samuel de Champlain followed, bringing with him four grey-robed Recollet friars of the Franciscan order. They were the first missionaries from France and were quickly followed by Jesuits, Sulpicians, Ursulines, and others.

While adventurers and explorers strove to monopolize the fur trade and the land, the missionaries spread their faith. Not surprisingly, the missionaries were often frustrated in their attempts to convert the indigenous peoples. Many of the missionaries gave their lives for their cause, such as the Jesuit priest Jean de Brébeuf and his fellow missionary, Gabriel Lalemant, who suffered a horrifying death at the hands of the Iroquois in 1649.

FIRST INDIGENOUS SAINT The first North American indigenous saint was Kateri Tekakwitha, known as the Lily of the Mohawks. Determined to live a life of virginity, she rejected several offers of marriage. This put her at odds with her people even before she was baptized a Christian in 1676. Persecuted by her people, Tekakwitha left for the Saint François-Xavier Mission in Quebec. She made a vow of chastity and became known for her sanctity. She died in 1680 and was beatified in 1980.

A 19th-century Protestant country church in Ontario.

CLAIMING THEIR OWN

As the European settlers opened up the continent of North America, the church became their constant companion and source of comfort in an undiscovered, hostile land. The English colonies were predominantly Protestant, while New France was Roman Catholic.

The French clergy faced great opposition in their attempts to convert the indigenous peoples, but they had it much easier among their own people. The French missionaries set up schools and hospitals, collected church tithes from the farmers, and had a powerful moral influence in French-Canadian society.

Marie Guyart, an Ursuline nun, came to Canada in 1639 and started a convent and school. She ministered to the leaders of New France and to indigenous girls, and earned herself the title of "spiritual mother of New France."

There were Anglican military and naval chaplains in Newfoundland and Nova Scotia before 1750. However, the thrust of Anglicanism in Canada came with the flood of Protestant Loyalist refugees who fled north during the American Revolution.

THE PIONEER CHURCH

Though seldom architecturally imposing, what the pioneer churches lacked in splendor they made up for in devotion. In the early days, there was seldom stone or materials for brick-making, but timber was abundant. The pioneer church was often built of wood, and many churches were made of logs. (It was the Swedes and Germans who introduced log cabin construction to Canada.)

The building of a church was a community event in which everyone would lend a hand. While the men worked to fell the trees, haul the logs, and put up the building, the women cooked to feed the team. When completed, the church became the hub of the settlers' lives. Sunday was a time when men could relax, women could socialize, and children could play, with everyone dressed in their finest.

ROOM FOR ALL BELIEFS

Other missionaries who came after the English and the French brought with them their own churches. The Dutch arrived with their Dutch Reformed Church. The Lutherans came from Sweden and Germany. The Scots introduced Presbyterianism when they emigrated to Nova Scotia in the 19th century.

Immigrants from Asia brought their own beliefs: Buddhism, Sikhism, Hinduism, and Islam. The empty lands of the prairies offered a refuge for a number of oppressed minority groups, among them the Mennonites, Ukrainians, Doukhobors, and Jews who left Russia for Canada. Today, there are many such small religious groups that have resisted pressures to change.

RELIGION AND MULTICULTURALISM

The Canadian emphasis on multiculturalism has also had its effect on religion. Canadians feel that people have a right to express their views but not to force their views on others. Canadians are tolerant of religious differences and not terribly enthusiastic about evangelism. Christian and non-Christian alike are free to practice their own forms of religion. Thus, while Christian churches of all denominations are a standard feature in Canada's towns and cities, mosques, synagogues, and temples are also common wherever there are communities of Canadians who practice those religions.

Saskatchewan Cree Chief Thunderchild in the late 19th century said: "The white men have offered us two forms of religion: the Roman Catholic and the Protestant. But we in our Indian bands have our own religion. Why is that not accepted too? It is the worship of one God, and it was the strength of our people for centuries."

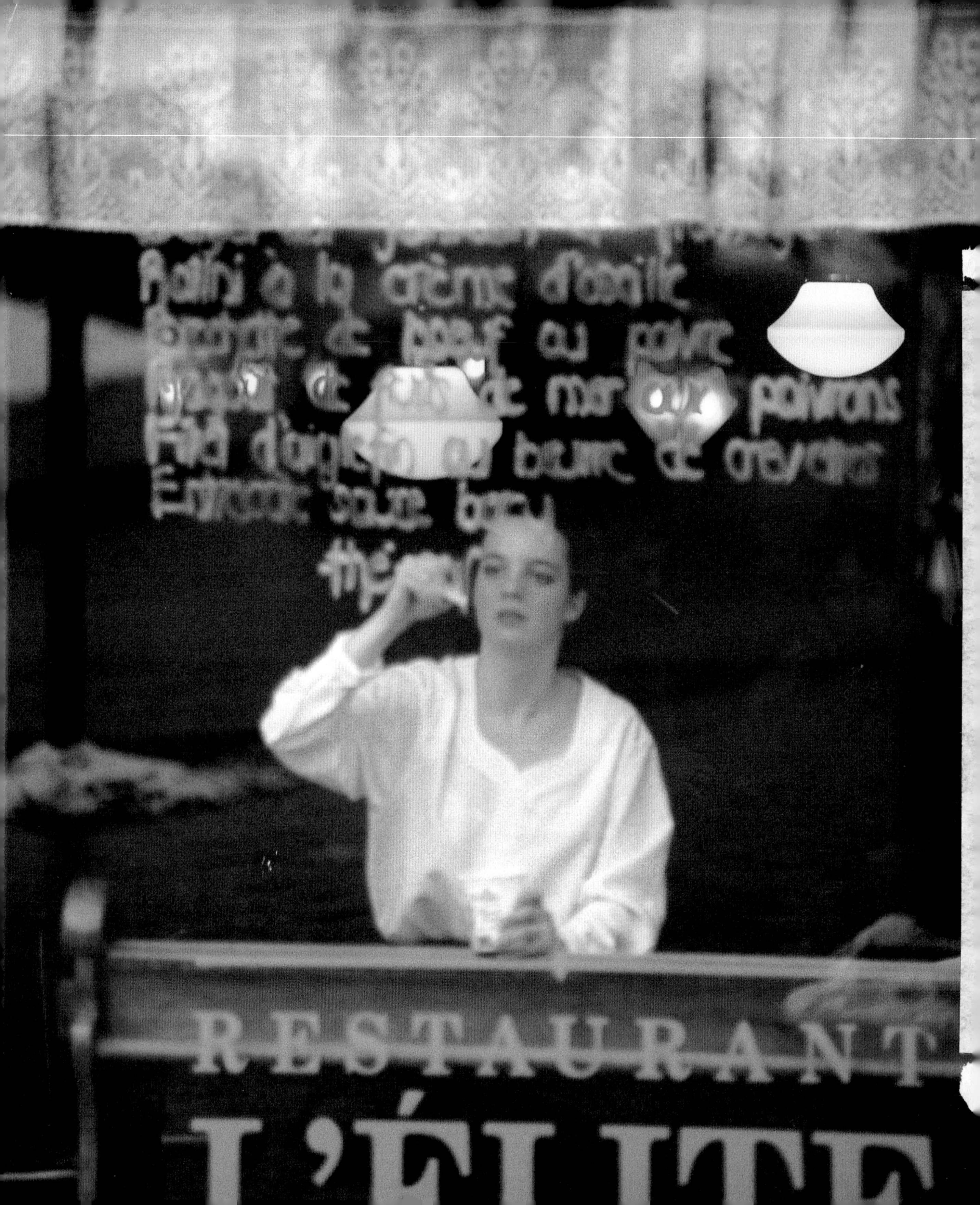
RESTAURANT
L'ÉLITE

LANGUAGE

EVERY CANADIAN has to study the country's two official languages, English and French. Sociologists and statisticians divide the Canadian population into a spectrum of francophones, anglophones, and allophones. A francophone is someone whose mother tongue is French. An anglophone is someone whose mother tongue is English. An allophone is someone whose mother tongue is neither English nor French.

DIVIDED BY TONGUES

The main languages spoken in Canada are English and French, because those are the languages of the original colonizers of the land. Today, the English-speaking community is distributed fairly evenly across Canada, while French-speaking Canadians are concentrated in the provinces of Quebec, New Brunswick, Ontario, and parts of Manitoba.

English is the mother tongue for most Canadians, except in Quebec, where most are francophone, and in the north, where many First Peoples speak their own languages. The proportion of Canadians who cite English as their mother tongue has been increasing since 1941 in all provinces except Quebec and Ontario. Ontario, which attracts many immigrants, has seen sharp growth in its allophone population since 1941. In 2001 Ontario had more than half of Canada's allophone population.

Other major languages are Dutch in Prince Edward Island, Greek in Quebec, German in Ontario, German and Ukrainian in Manitoba, Saskatchewan, and Alberta, and Chinese in British Columbia. Asian languages, especially Chinese, Vietnamese, Punjabi, Hindi, and Tagalog, have grown in prominence since the 1960s.

Opposite: **A restaurant employee writes out the day's menu in French in the French-Canadian city of Montreal.**

Below: **A sign in Ottawa shows Canada's widespread bilingualism.**

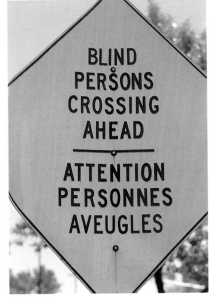

CANADIAN ENGLISH

English is the second most widely spoken language in the world. However, depending on where in the world it is being spoken, it can sound very different. Canadians too have their own brand of English. Think of Canadian English as a dialect resulting from both British and American influences as well as being distinctively Canadian.

Generations of immigrants from Britain are responsible for the British accents that are discernable in Canadian speech. Americans have also had great influence on Canadian English. Most of the differences that Americans notice in Canadian speech are due to the influence of the British, while British visitors notice that there are many features that are common to both American and Canadian English. This is true in both the spoken and written forms.

Canadians are comfortable switching between British and American terms and phrases. Sometimes they use them interchangeably. For instance, Canadians are just as likely to say taps and jam as they are to say faucets and jelly, which are more American. At the same time, Canadians may use the word fall in describing the season rather than the British term, autumn.

Differences in pronunciation are more

An indigenous-language and English bilingual sign at a Hudson's Bay Company station in the Northwest Territories.

obvious. For example, Canadians pronounce tomato, dance, half, and clerk the same way Americans do, but they pronounce been, lever, ration, and the letter Z like the British do.

Canadians do not always spell the way the British or Americans do either. Canadian spelling contains a mixture of British and American spellings. It uses British spelling for many words, such as behaviour, centre, and axe, and American spelling for some other words, such as program, sulfur, and authorize.

The almost uninterrupted flow of books and magazines, radio and television programs, and movies from south of the border and the movement and interaction of people both ways have given American English an increasing influence on Canadian speech, especially among the nation's youth.

This sign in a Toronto train station shows how English and French can be seen alongside each other on public notices.

LIRELIRE—a French bookshop in Montreal, Quebec.

CANADIAN FRENCH

French as spoken in Canada is not a patois (dialect) or a pidgin mixture of French, English, and an indigenous language. It is authentic French, brought to the country by the fewer than 10,000 original colonists who settled in New France in the 17th century. At that time, the French who came spoke various dialects, depending on their birthplace, but by the time the British took over the country with the Treaty of Paris in 1763, a Canadian brand of French had developed and had become the common language of the immigrants.

Cut off from their homeland, French Canadians developed a distinctly different language from that spoken in France. Increasingly under siege by a growing number of English-speaking newcomers, French Canadians resisted outside influence and developed a fierce pride that made them cling to their culture and language.

Today, French universities in Quebec do considerable research into the French language, and l'Académie Canadienne-Française, l'Office de la Langue Française, and le Ministère d'Affaires Culturelles are entrusted with the task of ensuring that Canadian French continues to flourish in the country.

LEARNING A SECOND LANGUAGE

Learning a second language is very important in Canada, because Canadians speak a variety of languages. English-speaking Canadians and immigrants to Quebec learn French as a second language. English is taught to francophones in Quebec and immigrants to English-speaking Canada. Either way, all Canadian schoolchildren study both English and French starting from elementary school. For non-native speakers of English, learning English as a second language is important for finding a job and being able to communicate with other Canadians.

But while a knowledge of French and English is important, under Canada's policy of multiculturalism, immigrants and indigenous peoples are encouraged to maintain knowledge of their own languages, called heritage languages, wherever learning facilities are available.

INDIGENOUS LANGUAGES

Anthropologists and linguists have classified the languages spoken by the indigenous peoples of Canada into 11 language families: Algonkian, Athapaskan, Iroquoian, Siouan, Kutenaian, Salishan, Wakashan, Tsimshian, Haida, Tlingit, and Eskimo-Aleut. The 11 families together consist of around 53 individual languages. Indigenous peoples belonging to the same language family do not necessarily share the same culture. For example, the Blackfoot of the plains and the Mi'kmaq of the Maritimes share a language that belongs to the Algonkian family, but their cultures are very different.

Of the indigenous languages that are still spoken in Canada, only three are widely used: Cree (Algonkian), Ojibway (Algonkian), and Inuktitut (Eskimo-Aleut). The others are in decline. Fortunately there is an increasing interest among the indigenous peoples themselves to try to preserve what remains by teaching their languages to their younger generations. The Northwest Territories government has encouraged the use of indigenous languages by adding six indigenous languages to its list of official languages.

The prevalence of both English and French is apparent in missing reports such as this one.

ARTS

CANADIAN ARTS reflect the diverse heritage of the nation's peoples. Where once it conveyed only the artistic perspective of the European colonizers, the Canadian arts scene has come to embrace the nation's indigenous cultures. The influence of the first peoples is seen and felt in many forms of contemporary Canadian art, from paintings to books to film. It appears that Canadian culture has returned to its roots in search of a way forward. At the same time, Canadians' growing pride in themselves and their achievements is reflected by a similar increase in uniquely Canadian art, literature, music, dramas, and movies.

INDIGENOUS ART

The indigenous arts existed in Canada centuries before the arrival of the Europeans. When the Europeans came, they influenced the development of the indigenous arts. For example, metal tools made it possible for indigenous artists, especially among the Inuit and peoples on the West Coast, to create more carved artifacts.

The arts were very much a part of daily life. Song, dance, and mime were used to summon the spirits for guidance and predictions of the future. Figures carved from bone, stone, or wood were thought to have magical qualities and helped to relay ancestral stories to the young. Pottery, basketry, and weaving produced everyday items, while drums were used in religious ceremonies. It was only when the Europeans discovered the indigenous works of art that indigenous artists began producing goods of commercial value.

Two well-known indigenous Canadian artists who have taken their art one step further are Robert Davidson, whose totem poles can be found in New York, Japan, and Switzerland, and the late Bill Reid, known for his incredible carvings.

Opposite: **Eye-catching wall art in Toronto.**

Below: **A house totem pole from the Northwest Territories. The eagle represents the Thunder Bird, which was believed to bring rain to prevent crops from withering.**

An exhibition hall of Canada's National Gallery in Ottawa. The gallery contains the country's most distinguished collection of Canadian and European paintings.

CANADIAN PAINTINGS

Early Canadian paintings were often romanticized depictions of Canadian life and land. Thomas Davies presented the beholder with pleasing and vivid but unreal watercolors of the Canadian landscape, while Paul Kane, who traveled from east to west to study and record the indigenous cultures, painted canvases that portrayed the indigenous peoples in an idealized and heroic manner.

Toward the end of the 19th century, it was Ozias Leduc of Quebec and James Wilson Morrice of Montreal who began to paint a distinctively Canadian landscape and lifestyle as they actually saw it. After their experiments came the works of Canada's most famous school of artists, the Group of Seven, which consisted of Lawren Harris, A. Y. Jackson, Arthur Lismer, Frederick Varley, Franklin Carmichael, Frank (Franz) Johnston, and J. E. H. MacDonald. They were inspired by the works of fellow Canadian Tom Thomson, an artist and outdoorsman. Nature was their theme, and they recorded the forms and colors of the northern Ontario landscape as never done before—brutal, rugged landscapes, rocks fractured and cracked by frost, trees blasted by fierce storms, and villages clinging to gullied slopes.

In the 1930s, a group of French-Canadian painters, including Alfred Pellan, Paul-Emile Borduas, Jacques de Tonnancour, and Jean-Paul Riopelle, painted in the modernist experimental style that was the trend in the art centers of Paris and New York.

Paintings by David Milne and Emily Carr are also considered Canadian classics. Carr, a West Coast artist, depicted the great forests of giant cedar and fir and was greatly influenced by the art of the indigenous peoples of the West Coast. She became the first woman artist to achieve fame in Canadian art. Later Canadian artists of note are Jack Shadbolt, another painter from western Canada who was similarly influenced by images of West Coast First Nations, and Robert Bateman, painter and celebrator of Canadian wildlife.

CANADIAN WRITERS

Early Canadian writers used a descriptive style and told stories of Canadian life. For example, sisters Susanna Moodie and Catharine Parr Traill, who came from a comfortable life in 19th-century England to a harsh one in the Canadian bush, described the hardships of their pioneer experience in Moodie's *Roughing it in the Bush* and *Life in the Clearings vs. the Bush* and Traill's *The Backwoods of Canada.* Satire found expression in the writings of Stephen Leacock, whose *Sunshine Sketches of a Little Town* (1912) was an ironic, humorous look at small-town Ontario provincial life. Thomas McCulloch's *Letters of Mephibosheth Stepsure* (1821–23) and Thomas Chandler Haliburton's *The Clockmaker: The Sayings and Doings of Samuel Slick of Slickville* (1836) are other humorous pieces.

The fame of *Anne of Green Gables,* a fictional story written by Prince Edward Island author Lucy Maud Montgomery about a lovable Canadian girl, has spread beyond Canada. Other modern Canadian writers who have achieved worldwide fame include Ethel Wilson, Hugh MacLennan, Alice Munro, Margaret Laurence, Margaret Atwood, Mordecai Richler, Robertson Davies, Morley Callaghan, and Leonard Cohen.

Caricaturists sell their skills and wares in the street. This one is of Queen Elizabeth II.

INDIGENOUS WRITERS The legends of the indigenous peoples are mostly in oral form. A hostile policy toward "Indians" encouraged the indigenous peoples to assimilate into the European population rather than celebrate their distinctiveness. But the 1970s proved a turning point when a great range of indigenous creative writing began to appear and then to flower in the 1980s. Some indigenous Canadian writers of note are Maria Campbell, Thomson Highway, Beatrice Culleton, Daniel David Moses, Jeannette Armstrong, Ruby Slipperjack, and Basil Johnston.

CANADA IN VERSE In the 1890s, Confederation was received with enthusiasm by the Confederation Poets, such as Bliss Carman, Charles Roberts, Archibald Lampman, and Duncan Campbell Scott. Roberts and Lampman wrote about rural life in the maritime provinces and

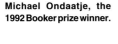

Michael Ondaatje, the 1992 Booker prize winner.

TEN BOOKS TO READ

There is much to learn about Canada—whether about life on the prairies or about the French-English dichotomy—from books written by Canadian writers. Here are some examples spanning the 20th century.

Lucy Maud Montgomery wrote *Anne of Green Gables* in 1908 about the adventures of a young and lovable Canadian girl. So popular has the book become that the Green Gables House, where Montgomery set the story of Anne, attracts thousands of tourists every year.

Morley Callaghan's *Such is My Beloved*, written in 1934, is a moving account of conflict between spiritual love and the realities of city living.

In 1947 W. O. Mitchell's *Who Has Seen the Wind?* painted a picture of life on the prairies, and Gabrielle Roy's *The Tin Flute* portrayed the clash between Anglo-American materialism and the old French order.

Mordecai Richler told the story of a young Jew from Montreal in *The Apprenticeship of Duddy Kravitz* in 1959.

Farley Mowat's *Never Cry Wolf* is a 1963 tale of the north. *The Stone Angel* (1964) is Margaret Laurence's powerful story about an elderly woman's struggle with the indignities of old age.

Anne Hébert's *Kamouraska*, written in 1970, was based on a real-life love-triangle murder that took place in Canada in 1840.

Margaret Atwood presented a frightening view of the future in *The Handmaid's Tale* (1985), while Thomas King took a humorous look at contemporary North American indigenous culture in *Green Grass, Running Water* (1993).

Ontario. Scott observed the northern indigenous peoples. In the 1930s, E. J. Pratt, A. J. M. Smith, F. R. Scott, and A. M. Klein expressed Canadian ideals and aspirations. Pratt wrote epics on historic themes, such as the missionary Brébeuf and the building of the Canadian Pacific. Smith's best-known poem on Canada is *The Lonely Land*, which celebrates the rugged, rocky, and wind-torn Canadian Shield. Scott and Klein took a broad humanistic and cosmopolitan view of Canada in the world.

Canada's modern poets include Michael Ondaatje, Phyllis Webb, Margaret Atwood, Leonard Cohen, and Alden Nowlan. Ondaatje in particular rose to fame when he won the British Booker prize in 1992 for his novel *The English Patient*.

An intermission at a playhouse in the Yukon.

PERFORMING ARTS

The film industry has become a valuable sector of the Canadian economy, especially in the two major film-making centers, Vancouver and Toronto. Canada's film industry brings in $5 billion in revenue each year. Low costs and the versatility of Vancouver and Toronto in transforming into American settings are reasons for the popularity of the two cities.

Most Canadian cities have small theaters that present the works of Canadian playwrights. The Canada Council for the Arts gives grants to theaters, opera and dance companies, orchestras, and arts councils in the various municipalities to help promote and support their activities. In the 1970s, hundreds of new Canadian plays were written, after the Canada Council insisted that at least half of the productions performed in Canadian theaters had to feature local content.

The Canadian music industry grew from a base of folk songs, dance tunes, and religious and patriotic music. Canadian singers and songwriters were major factors in the popularity of folk music in the 1960s. The 1970s and 1980s saw the rise of many Canadian rock groups. Some Canadian musicians and groups of note are Barenaked Ladies, Nelly Furtado, The Tragically Hip, and David Usher.

Symphony orchestras and dance companies can be found in almost every city. The annual Shakespeare Festival at Stratford, Ontario, and the Shaw Festival at Niagara-on-the-Lake, Ontario, are international events. Smaller towns and cities organize smaller-scale arts events. Arts-active people often get together and form their own choral, symphonic, and theatrical groups.

THE SHAKESPEARE FESTIVAL

The Stratford Festival of Canada at Stratford, Ontario, has gained an international reputation for its presentation of Shakespeare's plays. Stratford is considered to be one of the three great Shakespearean theaters of the English-speaking world, the other two being Britain's Royal Shakespeare Company and Royal National Theater. The Stratford Festival of Canada was started in 1953 by journalist Tom Patterson, with Tyrone Guthrie as its first artistic director. Today, the festival is celebrated in four theaters: the Tom Patterson Theater, which is used for workshops, experimental plays, and actor training; the 1,100-seat Avon Theater; the main 2,200-seat Festival Theater, which is a modern version of the traditional Elizabethan theater; and the new 260-seat Studio Theater. Around 600,000 people come to Stratford annually to enjoy classical and modern plays and music productions during the festival, which usually runs from April to November.

IN THE NEWS

Canada does not have a national newspaper or magazine. Every town has its own local newspaper, usually a weekly publication, covering events of interest to the community. Prominent daily newspapers, such as the *Vancouver Sun*, the *Toronto Star*, and the *Montreal Gazette*, are city publications and do not unite the communities of the provinces.

U.S. publications on sale in Canada.

Probably the closest thing Canada has to a national newspaper is *The Globe and Mail*, published in Toronto but distributed in all provinces.

Canada's own English-language news magazine is *Maclean's*, and its French-language equivalent is *L'Actualité*. Many Canadians read U.S. news magazines such as *Newsweek* and the Canadian edition of *Time*. A wide range of magazines published in Canada cater to a variety of interests. *Chatelaine* is a leading women's magazine covering health, fashion, love, and other areas of the modern Canadian woman's lifestyle, while *Saturday Night* offers something for everyone, from politics to art to entertainment.

The Canada Council for the Arts was created in 1957. Its function is to "foster and promote the study and enjoyment, and the production of works in, the arts." In order to do this, it gives grants to artists, organizations, and professional associations to help them in their cultural activities.

A NATIONAL IMAGE

Two media organizations that have done a lot to cultivate and present Canadian culture are the Canadian Broadcasting Corporation (CBC) and the National Film Board (NFB). The CBC is Canada's national radio and television service. It began as a Crown corporation, or government company, in 1936, inspired partly by the example of the British Broadcasting Corporation.

The CBC was also an attempt to counter the growing U.S. influence on Canadian radio. The CBC seeks to bring Canadians closer together by building stronger bonds between various communities through its programs. It provides news of national and international importance, as well as light and educational programs.

Right: **People line up to see some of the many U.S. movies shown in Canada.**

Opposite: **Raymond Massey, one of Canada's most illustrious stage and screen actors.**

John Grierson, a Scotsman, founded the NFB just before World War II. He had the task of creating a film company that could "interpret Canada to Canadians." The NFB nurtures emerging filmmakers and encourages innovative, creative productions. It has made many award-winning films and documentaries, teaching Canadians about their country.

THE GENIE AWARDS

The first Canadian Film Awards were presented in 1949 in Ottawa. The idea behind the awards was to promote Canadian artists and raise film standards. The last awards were given in 1978; in 1979, the Academy of Canadian Cinema was formed to continue this work. The academy presents the Genie Awards in more than 20 categories. Winners in the Best Motion Picture category include *Atanarjuat (The Fast Runner)* (2001) and *Ararat* (2002).

CANADIAN CONTENT

The federal government set up the Canadian Radio-Television and Telecommunications Commission (CRTC) to regulate the Canadian broadcasting and telecommunications industry. The CRTC lays down rules ensuring that Canadian radio and television broadcasts contain a substantial percentage of programs that are of Canadian origin. Under the Broadcasting Act, the objective of the CRTC is to ensure that all Canadians have access to a wide range of reasonably priced, high-quality, and creative Canadian programming that reflects the talent, multicultural and linguistic diversity, and social values of Canada. It also ensures that the indigenous peoples are well-represented.

LEISURE

THE AVERAGE CANADIAN works five days, 35 to 40 hours a week and gets at least two weeks' paid vacation and nine public holidays a year. It has been estimated that the average Canadian enjoys a minimum of 124 leisure days a year; many Canadians enjoy more.

Canadians spend a lot of their leisure time in the outdoors, enjoying the natural beauty of their country. However, they also watch a lot of television, especially sports programs, and spend 21.2 hours a week on average in front of the television.

SPORTS

Canadians are sports enthusiasts. There is a sport for almost any kind of weather, from 85°F (29°C) in summer to 20°F (-7°C) in winter. Many Canadian sports activities, such as tobogganing, snowshoeing, lacrosse, and canoeing, were introduced by the indigenous peoples.

The most important spectator sports in Canada are hockey, football, baseball, and basketball. Such sports are also a means for Canadians to display their national pride, cheering their teams on the playing field in international competitions.

LACROSSE This is the oldest Canadian game that is still played today. It was derived from a game called *baggataway*, which was played by the indigenous peoples as a means to develop group discipline and personal ingenuity.

When the French came to Canada, they liked the game so much that they developed it into lacrosse. The first lacrosse club was formed in Montreal in 1839. In 1867 the game became so popular that the National Lacrosse Association of Canada was formed, the first national sports organization in the country.

Opposite: **Skiing is one of the most popular winter sports in Canada.**

Ice hockey is a very physical game and is played with great passion in Canada.

HOCKEY In the Canadian context, hockey almost always means ice hockey rather than field hockey. Ice hockey is as Canadian as any game can get. It was invented by a group of Canadian soldiers in Kingston, Ontario, on a winter day in 1855. To relieve the monotony of garrison duty, the soldiers tied blades to their boots and hit an old lacrosse ball using field-hockey sticks.

Today, ice hockey unites all Canadians. Watching a hockey game on television or in the local arena has almost become a ritual. *Hockey Night in Canada* is the longest-running television program in the country—it first aired in 1952, which means that it has been running for more than 50 years.

Canadians learn to love hockey from a very early age. The moment school is out, bags are tossed aside and goal posts set up in the neighborhood cul de sac, where half a dozen kids or so clash with hockey sticks to put an old tennis ball into the net. In winter, the game is played on a frozen pond, stream, or indoor ice rink.

HOCKEY, THE RELIGION OF CONVENIENCE

Relating how hockey and the church helped to keep prairie communities together, Ken Dryden, author and former goalkeeper for the Montreal Canadiens, said in a television series on the game: "Hockey came later, the religion of convenience, linking communities together, town to town, region to region. For young and old, something to talk about, to share, a distraction from the long idle winters, a way to create and strengthen the community's bonds."

Canadian children often dream of becoming stars in the National Hockey League (NHL). Parents devote hours of their time taking aspiring NHL players to and from games and practices.

Canadian teams such as the Montreal Canadiens, the Edmonton Oilers, the Toronto Maple Leafs, and the Vancouver Canucks, as well as U.S. teams such as the Chicago Blackhawks and the Detroit Red Wings, are members of the NHL. In the NHL Hall of Fame are Canadians Maurice "Rocket" Richard, Bobby Orr, Bobby Hull, and Wayne Gretzky, also known as the Great One. Gretzky played for the Edmonton Oilers and the Los Angeles Kings before retiring in 1999 and is considered one of the greatest hockey players of all time.

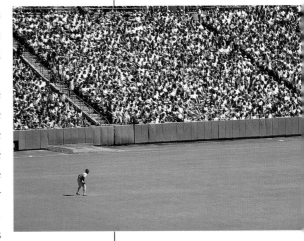

Crowds fill the stadium in Toronto to watch a baseball game.

BASEBALL Baseball is an American game that has captured a large Canadian following. Baseball diamonds are a necessary feature of playgrounds and parks in Canadian towns and cities. The game has been played in Canada professionally for more than a century. However, only two Canadian professional teams, the Toronto Blue Jays and the Montreal Expos, compete in the baseball leagues in the United States. As league members, they get to play in the World Series. In 1992, for the first time since the World Series began, the Toronto Blue Jays won the trophy. It was celebrated as a great Canadian victory, although the team's players had come from several countries.

The Toronto Sky Dome is the home of the Blue Jays. It was built at a cost of C$580 million and has a retractable roof that covers the stadium when the weather gets bad.

The skidoo or snowmobile is a Canadian invention. It is like a motorcycle and tractor combined with two skis in front and tracks behind. It provides the rider with the exhilaration and speed of motorcycling and the joys of playing in a winter wonderland.

CANADIAN FOOTBALL Football, a Canadian invention, was derived from the British game of rugby. Football was brought to Canada by immigrants and introduced to the United States by players from McGill University who played in Cambridge, Massachusetts, against a Harvard team. When they arrived in Cambridge, the McGill players found that Harvard played a version of soccer. To solve the problem, the teams played two games, each under the other's rules. The Harvard team liked the Canadian version so much that they introduced it to other teams in the United States. American football players soon introduced their own rules, thus creating American football. Canadian football has a slightly different set of rules from American football, and the game is played on a larger field, with 12 players a side instead of 11.

Football is played in high schools and colleges, but it is most popular in the big universities. The Canadian Football League (CFL) is the equivalent of the National Football League (NFL) in the United States. All the major cities in Canada have their own professional football teams, such as the Calgary Stampeders, the Ottawa Renegades, the Winnipeg Blue Bombers, the Edmonton Eskimos, and the BC Lions. American players are also allowed to play on Canadian teams.

BASKETBALL Created in 1891 by Canadian James Naismith, basketball has come to be a major part of the Canadian sports scene. Nearly every primary and secondary school in Canada has at least one basketball team, as do all of Canada's post-secondary institutions. Basketball courts can be found in many playgrounds and in most community centers. However, Canada has only one team in the National Basketball Association (NBA), the Toronto Raptors, since the Vancouver Grizzlies moved to Memphis, Tennessee, in 2001.

THE LURE OF THE WILD

For many Canadians, the wilderness is literally just outside the door. People who live in rural areas, or even in the suburbs of big cities, have access to parks and forests that are little more than minutes away. It is perhaps this proximity to nature that has made Canadians such an outdoor-loving people.

Canadians engage in a wide variety of outdoor activities that reflect Canada's physical geography. During the summer months, city dwellers migrate where possible to cottages, parks, and resorts scattered across the vast network of lakes and rivers for which Canada is justly famous. Canoeing, boating, hiking, and camping are popular from coast to coast.

Hunting and fishing are also popular activities all year round, but a license has to be obtained first. Hunters shoot many types of game, from small birds, such as grouse and ducks, to big animals, such as deer, bear, and moose. But there are special seasons for certain kinds of game and a limit to the number that a hunter can shoot. Sport fishing can be enjoyed on inland lakes and rivers as well as in the ocean. Ice fishing is also a popular winter pastime. Trout, salmon, and pike are just a few of the many types of fish available.

Skiing is almost the natural thing to do. Winters are comparatively long and almost certainly accompanied by snow. Skiing is possible where there are high hills and mountains. Downhill-ski resorts in the Western Cordillera of British Columbia and Alberta, and the Laurentian Highlands of Quebec, north of Montreal and Quebec City, are world-famous. British Columbia's renowned Whistler-Blackcomb ski resort will host many events in the 2010 Winter Olympics.

Skidooing or snowmobiling is a mechanical form of skiing.

NATIONAL AND PROVINCIAL PARKS

In order that Canadians may always enjoy the outdoors, there are many national and provincial parks, areas of wilderness preserved for the enjoyment of all. Canada named its first national park as early as 1885, when hot springs were discovered at Banff during the construction of the Canadian Pacific Railway. The Banff National Park in the Rocky Mountains was the first in an extensive national and provincial park system, which now includes more than 87,000 square miles (225,000 square km) of reserved land, including such diverse regions as the Pacific Rim National Park on the Pacific coast, the Point Pelee National Park in Ontario, and the Fundy National Park on the Atlantic coast, all managed by the federal government.

Many smaller provincial parks, managed by the provincial governments, dot Canada. Parks facilities vary. There are no roads in wilderness areas. Campers must leave their vehicles at the entrance to the parks and hike many miles inland, carrying all their camping

Fishing at one of the country's many national parks is a great way to relax.

LEARNING TO HUNT

Many schools and colleges teach a special course on outdoor recreation that prepares students who want to go hunting. In British Columbia, for instance, the course is called Conservation and Outdoor Recreation Education. Teenagers between ages 12 and 17 who wish to obtain their first BC resident hunting license or to use a gun must complete this course. It teaches students essential outdoor skills such as safety and survival techniques, how to handle firearms, and how to identity animals and birds. Hunting laws, regulations, and ethics are also taught.

equipment on their backs. In other parks, it is possible to drive right up to the campsite, which may accommodate either tents or large recreational vehicles. Some parks even have flush toilets and hot showers.

HOME ENTERTAINMENT

Most Canadians dream of owning their own home, and when they do own their own home, they spend a lot of leisure time improving it. Hidden in the basement or garage of many Canadian homes is a handy workshop filled with all kinds of mechanical and electrical tools.

At home, many Canadians engage in hobbies such as making handicrafts. The garden is another preoccupation. People look forward to the first frost-free day of the year to begin working outside, planting flowers or seeding a small vegetable garden.

Some leisure time is also spent watching television. Many homes have one or more stereo systems, a VCR or DVD player, a computer system, and a video-game console.

TRAVEL

Canadians love to travel and collectively spend a lot more money overseas than tourists who come to Canada do. The United States is the most popular destination, accounting for more than 80 percent of all trips abroad.

Canadians travel to the United States because it is so near and has many attractions and a larger selection of goods. Shopping was historically cheaper in the United States than in Canada, although the situation has changed with changes in currency values. Other favorite destinations among Canadians are Europe, the Caribbean, Mexico, Hong Kong, and Japan.

Enjoying the fresh air while watching a hockey game on television—an unusual mix of indoor and outdoor entertainment.

FESTIVALS

ON ANY DAY, somewhere in Canada, a festival or special event of some kind is bound to be taking place. It may be a celebration Canada shares with other countries, such as Christmas. Or it may be a Canadian event known all over the world, such as the Stratford Festival of Canada or the Calgary Stampede.

There are also many smaller-scale festivals, which have special significance to communities in different parts of the country. These festivals often celebrate the unique culture of a particular indigenous or immigrant group in Canadian society.

CHRISTMAS

Christmas is a major celebration for Christians in Canada. December 25 is traditionally celebrated as the birthday of Jesus Christ, but Santa Claus competes for center stage. Christmas in Canada is celebrated as much in the shopping malls as in the churches. Long before December, advertisements in newspapers and on radio and television remind people that they have to start shopping for Christmas gifts.

Family and friends gather for a Christmas dinner, most traditionally consisting of turkey, ham, and, less commonly, goose as well as mince pies and Christmas pudding. A Christmas tree trimmed with lights and decorations, with an angel or star on the top and wrapped gifts on the floor below, is an indispensable part of the festivities. Many Canadians also decorate their homes and gardens with outdoor lights to add color to this snow-white holiday.

For Christians, going to church is traditionally the focus of Christmas, especially on Christmas Eve and Christmas Day. The season is a joyous celebration of the coming of God's son, Jesus, to save the world.

Opposite: **A flag-raising ceremony held in Jasper, Alberta, on Canada Day.**

Below: **Ottawa's Caribbean people celebrate their heritage. A similar festival, called Caribana, takes place annually in Toronto.**

Canada's snowy winters are ideal for a classic white Christmas.

EASTER

Easter, observed in late March or early April, has retained more of its religious significance than has Christmas in Canada. Catholics prepare for Easter with the somber 40-day season of Lent. The end of Lent is marked by Good Friday, which recalls the suffering and death of Jesus Christ on the cross. Sorrow is replaced by joy on Easter Sunday, when according to Christian belief, Jesus Christ rose from the dead.

Hot-cross buns are associated with this time of the year. The small loaves of bread, spiced and sweetened, are marked with a cross on the surface. Chocolate Easter bunnies and Easter eggs originate in a pre-Christian tradition that held rabbits to be symbols of fertility and eggs of new life.

THANKSGIVING

Harvest time is a time of thanksgiving in Canada. Although people are becoming more removed from the land, they continue the tradition of giving thanks for a good harvest. In Canada, Thanksgiving falls on the second Monday of October, earlier than in the United States, where Thanksgiving falls on the fourth Thursday of November and is closely connected to the history of the Pilgrim Fathers.

Despite differences in date and reason, Canadians and Americans celebrate Thanksgiving in much the same way. Family members come home to be with one another and enjoy a Thanksgiving dinner of roast turkey with cranberry sauce, stuffing, potatoes, green vegetables, and a pumpkin pie for dessert.

HALLOWEEN

Halloween, or Hallow's Eve, is the eve of All Saints Day, which falls on November 1. On the night of October 31, young children look forward to dressing up in costumes and going from house to house yelling "trick or treat." Adults buy a lot of candy before Halloween and give it to the children to avoid having a trick played on them. Sometimes the elaborateness of the children's costumes is enough to earn them a treat. The younger children are often accompanied by their parents or older brothers and sisters on their trick-or-treat visits.

REMEMBRANCE DAY

On Remembrance Day, Canadians call to mind those who died while fighting in the two world wars and the Korean War. Canadians celebrate Remembrance Day, known as Veterans' Day in the United States, on November 11. The armistice that officially ended World War I took effect at the 11th hour of the 11th day of the 11th month—that is, 11 A.M. on November 11—in 1918.

On Remembrance Day, Canadians hold special ceremonies in towns and cities. Members of the Royal Canadian Legion, with other uniformed groups and service clubs, gather to honor and respect those who died serving the country. The Remembrance Day ceremony usually includes a recitation of *In Flanders Fields*, a poem by the late Colonel John McCrae of Guelph, Ontario.

Spooky pumpkin-headed scarecrows greet trick-or-treaters on Halloween. Hollowed out and carved with a grinning face, pumpkins also make glowing jack o' lanterns on Halloween.

CANADA DAY

Canada Day, formerly called Dominion Day, is celebrated on July 1, the anniversary of the creation of the Dominion of Canada in 1867. Towns and cities all over the country hold their own ceremonies on Canada Day to celebrate the unity of the country. The capital, Ottawa, hosts a large annual celebration that attracts Canadians from across the country. The year 1992 was special for Canadians, because it was the 125th birthday of the country. Encouraged by the government and the media, "Canada 125" celebrations took place all over the country. People expressed their love for their country in many ways, such as riding bicycles from coast to coast, creating a multi-patterned quilt to which many Canadians contributed a square, and planting trees.

CELEBRATING ORIGINS

Canadians come from diverse backgrounds. The multicultural character of Canadian society can be seen in the way people of different origins, religions, and traditions continue to celebrate these differences.

Long before the Europeans came to Canada, the indigenous peoples marked the year with festivals celebrating the seasons or religious rituals. The Ojibway had thanksgiving rituals in spring to celebrate the end of winter and in the fall for the bountiful harvest. The indigenous peoples of the West Coast held ceremonial feasts called potlatches, while those of the plains held lively cultural gatherings called powwows. In a more modern way, visitors who go to Brantford, Ontario, in August can take part in the Six

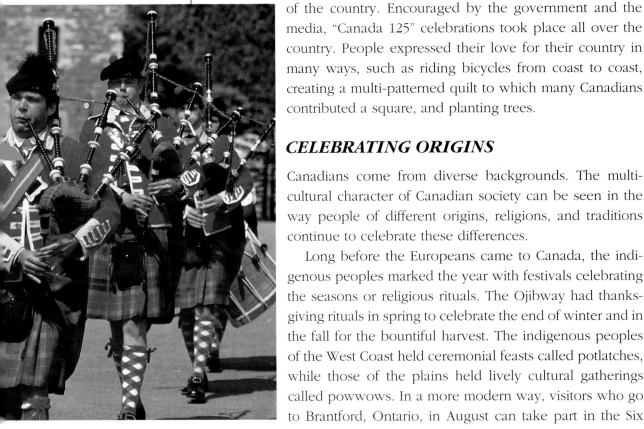

Montreal's Scottish community celebrates its origins with a bagpipe procession.

POWWOW

The word powwow comes from the old Algonquin word for medicine man. Today, powwows are inter-tribal gatherings that celebrate the rituals and spiritual beliefs of the indigenous peoples. The powwow is held over a number of days, during which there is almost nonstop sing-ing, dancing, and drumming, and a continuous parade of traditional and ceremonial indigenous dress and arts and crafts. Like the healing ceremonies performed by medicine men of the past, the powwow is a healing and unifying ritual that enables the indigenous peoples to show their pride in their culture.

Nations Native Pageant, an Iroquois celebration of the community's culture and history.

The oldest European immigrant groups in Canada hold festivals that display their foods, handicrafts, and lifestyles. The Festival du Voyageur in Saint Boniface, Winnipeg's French Quarter, celebrates the *joie de vivre,* or joy of life, of the region's early fur traders. In winter, Quebecers enjoy themselves at le Carnaval de Quebec. Scots-Canadians celebrate the annual Highland Games at Antigonish, Nova Scotia, and gather every four years in Nova Scotia for the International Gathering of the Clans.

Ukrainians in the town of Dauphin, Manitoba, hold a National Ukrainian Festival, which showcases Ukrainian costumes, artifacts, and fiddling contests. The Vesna Festival, in Saskatoon, Saskatchewan, is another Ukrainian festival of foods and handicrafts. The Pioneer Days Parade in Steinbach, Manitoba, celebrates Mennonite heritage with a display of threshing, baking, and food samples. The large Chinese community in Vancouver, British Columbia, celebrates the Chinese New Year with dragon dances and firecrackers.

At a rodeo competition at the Calgary Stampede, a cowboy tries to see how long he can ride a bucking wild horse before he is thrown off.

THEME FESTIVALS

Communities all over Canada create celebrations relating to the history or special attractions of an area. Such celebrations develop community spirit and pride. For example, many towns in the cattle-ranching regions have rodeos during which cowboys display their skills and talents. The most famous cowboy festival is the Calgary Stampede in July, complete with chuck-wagon and hot-air balloon races, rodeo showmanship, and agricultural and handicraft displays.

Many festivals provide a showcase for music, art, drama, handicrafts, and sports. The town of Banff in the Rocky Mountains holds a summer-

THE OKANAGAN WINE FESTIVAL

The Okanagan Wine Festival started in 1980 with only a handful of wineries. Today there are more than 30, and the number is growing. The festival is so popular with tourists, it is held twice a year. As part of the festivities, a grape-stomp annual championship is held in which teams of people squash tons of grapes with their feet, cheered on by hundreds of spectators. Wineries uncork their finest products for tasting by a thirsty public.

long Festival of the Arts, which attracts thousands of musicians, singers, dancers, and artists. Edmonton has an annual street performers' festival in July and a Folk Music Festival and Fringe Theater Festival in August. Montreal hosts its International Film Festival every summer.

The seasons of the year provide an excellent theme for celebration. Spring is the reason for the Annapolis Valley Apple Blossom Festival, the Maple Syrup Festival in Plessisville, Quebec, and the Ottawa Tulip Festival. In summer, the pace of festivities picks up with the warmer weather. Jazz festivals in Montreal, Toronto, and Vancouver, along with the Vancouver International Comedy Festival, attract Canadians and foreign tourists alike.

HOLIDAYS

Many Canadian public holidays fall on a Friday or a Monday so that people can enjoy a long weekend. This is important in such a large country, where people are very mobile and must travel long distances in order to be with their families. Many Canadians enjoy these holidays:

- New Year's Day, January 1.
- Good Friday and Easter Monday (dates vary according to the Christian calendar).
- Victoria Day, which celebrates Queen Victoria's birthday, May 24 or the Monday preceding it.
- Saint Jean Baptiste Day is the day of the patron saint of Quebec, celebrated on June 24 (only in Quebec).
- Canada Day, July 1, celebrated everywhere except in Quebec. In Newfoundland and Labrador, it is known as Memorial Day and is observed on the Monday nearest July 1.
- Labor Day, the first Monday in September, is celebrated everywhere except in Prince Edward Island. It is the last holiday of the summer season, after which school resumes.
- Thanksgiving, the second Monday in October.
- Christmas Day, December 25.
- Boxing Day, December 26, a time when gifts are given to those who have provided services throughout the year.

FOOD

CANADIAN FOOD is difficult to define. In many ways it is undistinguished. In fast-food restaurants in towns and cities, one can eat one's fill of hot dogs, hamburgers, and french fries. The menu of a café or restaurant is filled with similar food, plus the standard soups, main courses of meat, potatoes, and vegetables, and ice-cream and pie desserts.

One handbook for university students describes the basic Canadian meal as: "… meat and potatoes plus other vegetables. Eggs, cheese, and fish are common meat substitutes, while spaghetti, noodles, and rice or beans are a few common substitutes for potatoes. Vegetables and fruit are included in most meals. Generally speaking, Canadians do not spice their food heavily." Fortunately, this is not the complete picture. Canadian food is tremendously varied, consisting of the variety of cuisines that came with the different peoples who settled in Canada over time.

A bishop in Yukon, Isaac O. Stringer, discovered that when one is starving one will eat anything. Back in 1909, he and his companion became lost but survived their ordeal, thanks to their sealskin boots, which they boiled and toasted!

Opposite: **An employee of the Boulangerie Première Moisson, a bakery in Atwater Market, Montreal.**

Left: **A Canadian family at mealtime.**

Cod being unloaded in New Brunswick.

THE BOUNTY OF THE SEA

Nearly 9 percent of Canada is covered with water. Lakes and rivers all over the country contain abundant fish. In the Atlantic provinces of Newfoundland, Prince Edward Island, Nova Scotia, and New Brunswick, fish, especially cod, is available all year round. It is first dried, pickled, or salted, and then eaten cooked in different ways.

In Newfoundland, seal flipper pie is a speciality. To make it, you have to scrape off the hair and cut off the blubber from seal's flippers, simmer the flippers for a long time, add pork and flour to make a stew-like mixture, and cover the mixture with pastry. Another popular dish of Newfoundlanders is boiled salted pork or beef with potatoes, turnips, carrots, and cabbage.

The food of Nova Scotia reflects the cuisines of the Scottish, English, German, Swiss, and French settlers in the province. Examples of Nova Scotia dishes are fish chowder, Lunenburg sausage with sauerkraut, and Solomon Gundy, which consists of cured herring fillets mixed with a special blend of spices and onions.

New Brunswick is known for its clam chowder, made with the large clams of the Shediac region. Dulse is another offering of the sea. It is an edible seaweed that grows on the rocks in the North Atlantic and Northwest Pacific oceans, and is harvested along the shores of New Brunswick and Nova Scotia and of islands such as the Grand Manan.

The oysters of Prince Edward Island's Malpeque Bay are used to make a rich soup called oyster bisque, while fresh lobsters are often steamed, boiled, added to salads, or made into delicious lobster thermidor and accompanied by PEI's famous potatoes.

HAUTE CUISINE

Everybody knows that the French and good food go together; the same applies to French-Canadians. Few would disagree that the two best cities in Canada for good French restaurants are Montreal and Quebec City. Many restaurants in these cities used to serve mainly fancy French food, or *haute cuisine*, such as *paté de foie gras* (an appetizer made of goose liver) or *coq au vin* (chicken simmered in Burgundy wine), but traditional French-Canadian country food has found its place on their menus too. Restaurants in Quebec have added to their menus a meat pie called *tourtière*, maple syrup sugar pie made with real maple sugar, cretons (a meat spread for sandwiches), and Oka cheese, among other local dishes.

COSMOPOLITAN ONTARIO

Ontario, especially Toronto, is one of Canada's most cosmopolitan regions. Half of Toronto's residents were born outside the country. Immigrants have given the province a special flavor in terms of food, from solid English steak and kidneys to delicate Italian capellini.

The British preserved their love for creamed kippers and minced lamb pie even as they learned to appreciate more exotic foods. Italians, mainly from southern Italy, opened shops selling blocks of Parmesan cheese, bins full of olives, and vegetables such as artichokes and zucchini. Hungarians, Yugoslavs, Poles, and Rumanians added their own variations of dumplings, stews, and sauerkraut.

A night out for *haute cuisine* in some of Quebec's more expensive French restaurants.

PICK YOUR OWN

Some farms and orchards encourage people to pick their own fruit. This is advertised on a roadside sign. Many people love to make a family outing out of harvesting their own fruit from a nearby farm. By picking your own, you see to it that you get just what you want. There is a certain etiquette that should be followed. Most farmers do not mind if you eat some fruit while picking, but you should not put more in your mouth than in the bucket. Children are welcome, but parents should ensure that their children do not disturb other pickers or run around. If you have never picked your own fruit, the farmer will gladly show you the best way of doing it, which varies according to the fruit.

NORTHERN COUNTRY FOODS

Wild game forms a large part of the diet in the north, where people still hunt, fish, and trap for food. Country foods remain the staple diet of the northern indigenous peoples, partly because they are more economical than food sold in stores. Country foods are also recognized as being healthier than processed food.

The indigenous peoples traditionally hunt big animals such as moose and caribou in large groups. They share the meat in their families and communities as a way of reinforcing kinship and bonds. Smaller game such as waterfowl, rabbits, and sheep are hunted in smaller groups. Indigenous groups that live in the west fish for salmon, which is smoked and dried. Groups along the coast fish for arctic char and cod and hunt whales, seals, and walruses. Inuit also hunt polar bears for their hide, fat, and flesh.

In summer, indigenous peoples gather berries, blueberries probably being the most popular. They also gather root vegetables to supplement their diet. Indigenous peoples in some areas use wood chips from cedar, maple, and hickory trees, and even pine cones to flavor their food.

THIRST QUENCHERS

Canadians drink tea and coffee in the morning, after meals, and all day long. Children consume milk, fruit juices, and chocolate-flavored drinks. Carbonated soft drinks—or pop, as Canadians call them—such as Coca-Cola, 7-Up, and of course Canada Dry, are available everywhere. Bottled water is growing in popularity among Canadians, and Canada's bottled water industry is heavily regulated to ensure the purity of its waters.

Canada produces its own wine, beer, and whisky. There are two main wine-producing regions: southwestern Ontario, especially the Niagara region, and the Okanagan area in the interior of British Columbia. Several large manufacturers produce many brands of Canadian beer. There are also small local breweries called microbreweries, which sell their beer through special brew-pubs.

EATING ORGANIC

Eating right is increasingly important for many Canadians who believe in the saying that you are what you eat. A large part of this focus is an interest in organic foods, meaning food that has not been genetically modified or treated with chemicals such as pesticides or steroids.

Pesticides are a growing concern. They are widely used in farming and have been found to be bad for our health. Similarly, steroids used by farmers to increase yields in cattle, chickens, pigs, and dairy products have been shown to have adverse side-effects. Of special concern is the use of antibiotics in farm animals. That can produce antibiotic-resistant bacteria in human consumers, which are a serious threat to health. Canada is a large producer of genetically modified crops, especially canola, even though this relatively new biotechnology is extremely controversial.

In some cities, organic foods have reached such a level of popularity that there are large grocery stores dedicated entirely to providing a wide variety of organic produce and meats. Serving organic foods is a popular feature in many cafés and restaurants. Growing organic produce and raising free-range steroid-free livestock have become valuable sectors of Canada's agricultural production.

MAPLE SYRUP

Maple syrup is harvested in both Quebec and Ontario in the early springtime, when the days are warm and the nights are cold. This is the time when the sap of the maple tree rises from the roots and can be tapped.

Mature maple trees are tapped by driving a spigot into the side of the tree. A bucket or plastic tube is attached to the spigot to collect the sap, which is sweet but thin. In order to make just a gallon of syrup, about 40 times more sap has to be collected.

The maple tree sap is put in special containers and boiled until it becomes sufficiently thick. Sugaring off, as the boiling process is called, is a great social event. Children in particular love it, because they get to enjoy a special treat called sugar on snow—chewy bits of toffee made by splashing some of the hot, thick maple syrup onto clean snow on the ground.

Canadians of all ages love sugaring off.

FOOD BANKS

Most people in Canada have plenty to eat, but there are also people who do not have enough money to feed themselves and their families. Charitable organizations and volunteer groups try to do something for the less fortunate by running food banks.

The Canadian Food Bank Association estimates that the food banks, which provide free meals and groceries to the needy, dish out about 2.1 million meals every month.

A BC MIX

Chinese, Japanese, Indians, and other Asians in Canada form large, visible minorities in the province of British Columbia, especially in Vancouver. They have added their exotic foods to Canadian cuisine. Asian foods such as tofu, noodles, and curry, and spices such as cumin and cardamom can commonly be found on supermarket shelves in British Columbia.

British Columbia is also known for the variety and quality of its fish. There are five varieties of Pacific salmon: chum, coho, pink, sockeye, and chinook. Huge quantities of salmon are caught every year in the province. They reach the markets fresh, smoked, or canned. The abundance of salmon and other fish along the West Coast, together with the presence of many Asian-born residents and visitors, has made Vancouver one of the world's best locations for delicious and amazingly affordable sushi.

The market gardens and orchards of British Columbia produce a wealth of fruit, including peaches, pears, plums, melons, berries, and apples. Loganberries and giant Zucca melons are two special fruits seldom found anywhere outside the province. Loganberries, a cross between raspberries and blackberries, are cultivated on Vancouver Island.

BANNOCK

Recipes for aboriginal bread have evolved over the years, varying across communities and according to the availability of ingredients. Corn flour or cornmeal is the usual main ingredient, although wheat flour is a good substitute. This bannock recipe is one of many.

1 cup plain or all-purpose flour
½ teaspoon baking powder
¼ teaspoon salt
3 tablespoons vegetable oil
⅓ cup water
Oil for frying

Mix the flour, baking powder, and salt. Add the vegetable oil, and mix well. Add the water, and knead well to form a dough. Heat some oil in a frying pan. When it is hot, spread the dough in the pan, and fry until golden brown. Serve hot. Spread with jam, bannock makes an excellent breakfast. Add dried fruit such as raisins for variety.

NANAIMO BAR

This dessert, extremely popular on the West Coast, is best enjoyed in small portions. This recipe makes 24 bars. Covered and refrigerated, they can keep for a month. They can also be frozen.

2 cups graham cracker crumbs
$^1/_2$ cup chopped walnuts
2 tablespoons sugar
1 cup shredded coconut
1 teaspoon vanilla
1 egg
2 ounces (57 g) melted semi-sweet chocolate

$^3/_4$ cup softened butter
3 tablespoons milk
2 tablespoons instant vanilla pudding
2 cups confectioner's sugar
4 ounces (113 g) semi-sweet chocolate
1 tablespoon butter

Combine the crumbs, nuts, and 2 tablespoons sugar. Combine the coconut, vanilla, egg, melted chocolate, and $^1/_2$ cup softened butter. Mix the two parts, then press into a 9-inch (23-cm) square cake pan to form a base. Chill. Combine the milk, vanilla pudding, and $^1/_4$ cup softened butter. Blend in the confectioner's sugar, then spread over the base. Chill for at least 15 minutes. Partially melt 4 ounces chocolate and 1 tablespoon butter. Remove from the heat and stir until melted. Spread over the second layer in the pan, then chill again. Cut into 24 equal bars. Serve chilled.

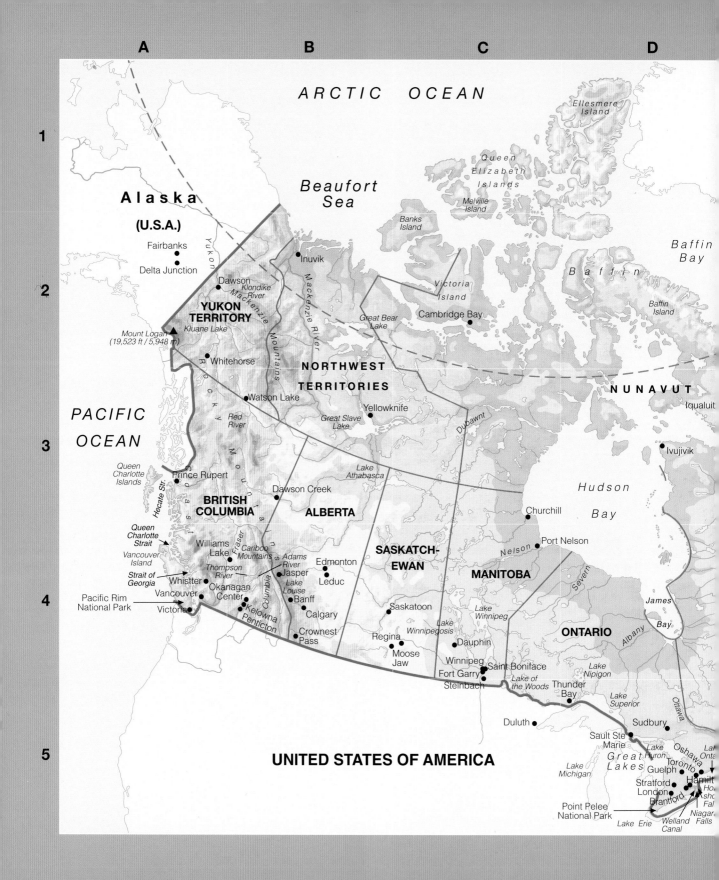

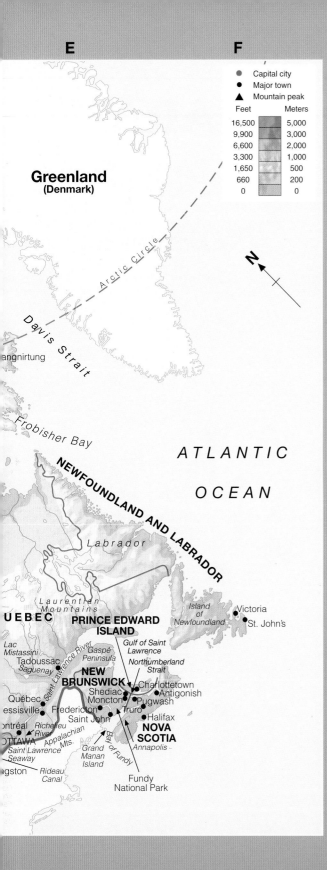

MAP OF CANADA

ECONOMIC CANADA

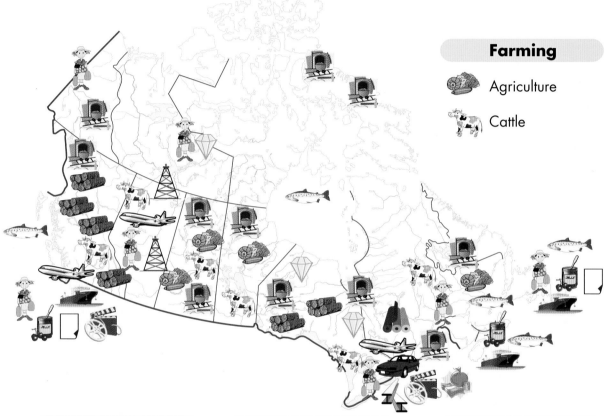

Farming

 Agriculture

Cattle

Services

Airport

Filmmaking

Finance

Port

Tourism

Manufacturing

Automobiles

Food Products

Pulp & Paper

Steel

Textiles

Natural Resources

Diamond

Fish

Forestry

Oil

Other Minerals

ABOUT
THE ECONOMY

OVERVIEW
Natural resources have been Canada's economic backbone since its earliest days. While oil, natural gas, mining, and forestry are vital sectors, manufacturing and services have become the mainstay of the Canadian economy, and tourism is growing in importance.

GROSS DOMESTIC PRODUCT (GDP)
US$715.7 billion (2002)

GDP SECTORS
Services 71 percent, industry 27 percent, agriculture 2 percent (2002)

NATURAL RESOURCES
Potash, uranium, zinc, aluminum, nickel, cadmium, gypsum, asbestos, copper, titanium, platinum, salt, gold, molybelenum, cobalt, lead, silver

LAND AREA
3.9 million square miles (9,976,000 square km)

CURRENCY
1 Canadian dollar (CAD) = 100 cents
Notes: 5, 10, 20, 50, 100, 1,000 dollars
Coins: 1, 5, 10, 25 cents; 1, 2 dollars (loonie and toonie respectively)
USD 1 = CAD 1.40 (May 2004)

INFLATION RATE
2.2 percent (2003)

WORKFORCE
17.1 million (2003)

WORKFORCE BY OCCUPATION
Services 74 percent, manufacturing 15 percent, construction 6 percent, agriculture 2 percent

UNEMPLOYMENT RATE
7.6 percent (2003)

AGRICULTURAL PRODUCTS
Wheat, barley, oats, fruit, vegetables, dairy products, fish, oilseed, canola, forest products

INDUSTRIAL PRODUCTS
Motor vehicles and parts, industrial machinery, aircraft, telecommunications equipment, crude petroleum, natural gas, timber, wood pulp and paper, aluminum, chemicals, plastics

MAJOR TRADE PARTNERS
The United States, Japan, the United Kingdom, Germany, China, Mexico, South Korea, France

MAJOR EXPORTS/IMPORTS
Petroleum, natural gas, chemicals, minerals, motor vehicles and parts, industrial equipment, agricultural products, food products, wood and paper products

MAJOR PORTS AND HARBORS
Vancouver, Toronto, Montreal, Halifax, Saint John's

CULTURAL CANADA

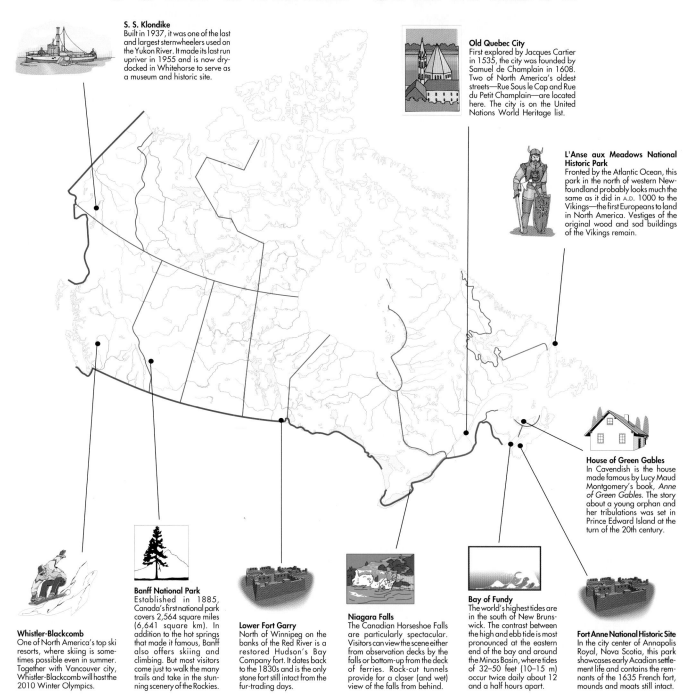

S. S. Klondike
Built in 1937, it was one of the last and largest sternwheelers used on the Yukon River. It made its last run upriver in 1955 and is now dry-docked in Whitehorse to serve as a museum and historic site.

Old Quebec City
First explored by Jacques Cartier in 1535, the city was founded by Samuel de Champlain in 1608. Two of North America's oldest streets—Rue Sous le Cap and Rue du Petit Champlain—are located here. The city is on the United Nations World Heritage list.

L'Anse aux Meadows National Historic Park
Fronted by the Atlantic Ocean, this park in the north of western New-foundland probably looks much the same as it did in A.D. 1000 to the Vikings—the first Europeans to land in North America. Vestiges of the original wood and sod buildings of the Vikings remain.

House of Green Gables
In Cavendish is the house made famous by Lucy Maud Montgomery's book, *Anne of Green Gables*. The story about a young orphan and her tribulations was set in Prince Edward Island at the turn of the 20th century.

Whistler-Blackcomb
One of North America's top ski resorts, where skiing is some-times possible even in summer. Together with Vancouver city, Whistler-Blackcomb will host the 2010 Winter Olympics.

Banff National Park
Established in 1885, Canada's first national park covers 2,564 square miles (6,641 square km). In addition to the hot springs that made it famous, Banff also offers skiing and climbing. But most visitors come just to walk the many trails and take in the stun-ning scenery of the Rockies.

Lower Fort Garry
North of Winnipeg on the banks of the Red River is a restored Hudson's Bay Company fort. It dates back to the 1830s and is the only stone fort still intact from the fur-trading days.

Niagara Falls
The Canadian Horseshoe Falls are particularly spectacular. Visitors can view the scene either from observation decks by the falls or bottom-up from the deck of ferries. Rock-cut tunnels provide for a closer (and wet) view of the falls from behind.

Bay of Fundy
The world's highest tides are in the south of New Bruns-wick. The contrast between the high and ebb tide is most pronounced at the eastern end of the bay and around the Minas Basin, where tides of 32–50 feet (10–15 m) occur twice daily about 12 and a half hours apart.

Fort Anne National Historic Site
In the city center of Annapolis Royal, Nova Scotia, this park showcases early Acadian settle-ment life and contains the rem-nants of the 1635 French fort, mounds and moats still intact.

ABOUT THE CULTURE

OFFICIAL NAME
Canada

CAPITAL
Ottawa

OTHER MAJOR CITIES
Calgary, Edmonton, Montreal, Quebec City, Toronto, Vancouver, Victoria, Saskatoon, Regina, Winnipeg, Halifax, Saint John's

PROVINCES AND TERRITORIES
Alberta, British Columbia, Manitoba, New Brunswick, Newfoundland, Northwest Territories, Nova Scotia, Nunavut, Ontario, Prince Edward Island, Quebec, Saskatchewan, Yukon

GOVERNMENT
Confederation with parliamentary democracy

NATIONAL FLAG
Eleven-point red maple leaf on white, framed by red bars.

NATIONAL ANTHEM
O Canada. Adopted July 1, 1980. Music by Calixa Lavallée (1880), French lyrics by Sir Adolphe-Basile Routhier (1880), English lyrics by Justice Robert Stanley Weir (1908, modified 1968). (To listen, go to www.pch.gc.ca/progs/cpsc-ccsp/sc-cs/anthem_e.cfm)

POPULATION
31,629,700 (2003)

MAJOR ETHNIC GROUPS
European descent (English 20 percent, French 16 percent, Scottish 14 percent, Irish 13 percent, German 9 percent, Italian 4 percent), Chinese 3.7 percent, aboriginal 3.4 percent (2001)

RELIGIOUS GROUPS
Roman Catholics 43 percent, Protestants 30 percent, other Christians 4 percent; Muslims 2 percent; Jews, Hindus, Sikhs, Buddhists 4 percent (2001)

OFFICIAL LANGUAGES
English and French

LITERACY RATE
99 percent (1995)

HOLIDAYS AND IMPORTANT ANNIVERSARIES
New Year's Day (January 1), Good Friday and Easter (March/April), Canada Day (July 1), Thanksgiving (2nd Monday in October), Remembrance Day (November 11), Christmas (December 25)

LEADERS IN POLITICS
Paul Martin—Liberal Party leader, prime minister (since December 2003)
Adrienne Clarkson—governor-general (since 1999)
Jean Chrétien—prime minister (1993–2003)
Pierre E. Trudeau—prime minister, oversaw repatriation of constitution (1968–79, 1980–84)
Lester B. Pearson—prime minister, Nobel Peace Prize winner (1963–68)

TIME LINE

IN CANADA	IN THE WORLD

10,000 B.C.
Indigenous groups spread over Canada.

753 B.C.
Rome is founded.

116–17 B.C.
The Roman Empire reaches its greatest extent, under Emperor Trajan (98–17).

A.D. 500
Indigenous groups develop extensive social and economic links.

A.D. 600
Height of Mayan civilization

992
Leif Ericsson explores Newfoundland.

1000
The Chinese perfect gunpowder and begin to use it in warfare.

1530
Beginning of trans-Atlantic slave trade organized by the Portuguese in Africa.

1534
Jacques Cartier discovers the Saint Lawrence River.

1603
Samuel Champlain explores the Great Lakes.

1558–1603
Reign of Elizabeth I of England

1620
Pilgrims sail the *Mayflower* to America.

1632
Champlain is appointed the first governor.

1763
France recognizes British claims to Canada and cedes Nova Scotia.

1774
Quebec Act upholds French civil law.

1776
U.S. Declaration of Independence

1791
Upper and Lower Canada are created.

1789–99
The French Revolution

1841
Act of Union creates the Province of Canada.

1858
Ottawa is chosen as Canada's capital.

1861
The U.S. Civil War begins.

1867
Union of Canada

1869
The Suez Canal is opened.

IN CANADA	IN THE WORLD

1870–73
Northwest Territories, British Columbia, Manitoba, and Prince Edward Island join Canada.

1903
The United States is given the Alaskan Panhandle.

1905
Alberta and Saskatchewan join Canada.

1920
Canada joins the League of Nations.

1945
Canada becomes one of the founding members of the United Nations.

1949
Newfoundland joins Canada.
Canada joins NATO.

1960
Indigenous Canadians win the right to vote.

1982
Quebec withholds agreement on the Constitution Act of 1982.

1987–92
Two attempts to resolve the constitution issue fail.

1995
Quebecois vote to remain part of Canada.

1999
The territory of Nunavut is created.

2003
Paul Martin succeeds Jean Chrétien as Liberal Party leader and prime minister.

1914
World War I begins.

1939
World War II begins.

1945
The United States drops atomic bombs on Hiroshima and Nagasaki.

1949
The North Atlantic Treaty Organization (NATO) is formed.

1957
The Russians launch Sputnik.

1966–69
The Chinese Cultural Revolution

1986
Nuclear power disaster at Chernobyl in Ukraine

1991
Break-up of the Soviet Union

1997
Hong Kong is returned to China.

2001
Terrorists crash planes in New York, Washington, D.C., and Pennsylvania.

2003
War in Iraq

GLOSSARY

baggataway
An indigenous game played to develop group discipline and personal ingenuity.

bannock
A bread originating from the indigenous groups. It is usually made from cornmeal.

Calgary Stampede
A famous Canadian festival of rodeos and races held every July in Calgary, Alberta.

Confederation
The union of New Brunswick, Nova Scotia, and the Province of Canada in 1867, forming the Dominion of Canada. Included the Northwest Territories in 1870, British Columbia in 1871, Prince Edward Island in 1873, Yukon in 1898, Newfoundland in 1949, and Nunavut in 1999.

Crown land
Canadian land belonging to the public and administered by the government.

First Nations
The name by which Canada's aboriginal peoples would like to be known.

Inuit
An aboriginal people, previously called Eskimos, who inhabit the northern, Arctic areas of Canada and Greenland.

kayak
A light boat traditionally made of sealskin.

Maritimes
The collective name for the provinces of Prince Edward Island, Nova Scotia, and New Brunswick.

Mountie
An officer of the Royal Canadian Mounted Police.

New France
The name of French-controlled North America until 1763, encompassing a part of present-day United States and Canada.

potlatch
An indigenous ceremonial feast.

powwow
An indigenous cultural gathering or festival.

prairie
An open, grass-covered, treeless landscape. The Canadian prairies cover the southern parts of Alberta, Saskatchewan, and Manitoba.

shaman
A medicine man believed to be able to communicate with the spirits and heal the sick.

teepee
A tent made of animal skins stretched over a framework of poles.

territories
Federally governed regions with smaller populations than the provinces. Canada has three: Yukon, the Northwest Territories, and Nunavut.

FURTHER INFORMATION

BOOKS

Barlas, Bob and Norman Tompsett. *Canada*. Milwaukee: Gareth Stevens Publishing, 1999.

Boraas, Tracey. *Canada*. Countries and Cultures series. Mankato: Bridgestone Books, 2002.

Colombo, John Robert. *Only in Canada: A Treasury of Canadian Humour*. Toronto: Colombo & Company, 2002.

Dawood, Ishie. *Canada: A History to the 20th Century*. Edmonton: Reidmore Books, 1992.

Grabowski, John F. *Canada*. Modern Nations of the World series. San Diego: Lucent Books, 1998.

Law, Kevin. *Canada*. Philadelphia: Chelsea House Publishers, 1998.

Nickles, Greg and Niki Walker. *Canada*. Nations of the World series. Austin: Raintree Steck-Vaughn, 2000.

Park, Ted. *Taking Your Camera to Canada*. Austin: Steadwell Books, 2000.

WEBSITES

Calgary Stampede. www.calgarystampede.com

Canada.com (up-to-date Canadian news and information). www.canada.com

The Canada Council for the Arts. www.canadacouncil.ca

Canada's Online Information Source. www.cbc.ca

Canadian Biosphere Reserves Association. www.biosphere-canada.ca

The Canadian Film Center. www.cdnfilmcentre.com/index1.html

Central Intelligence Agency World Factbook (select Canada from the country list).
www.cia.gov/cia/publications/factbook

Government of Canada. www.gc.ca

Government of Canada YouthPath. www.youth.gc.ca

Hockey Canada. www.hockeycanada.ca

Lonely Planet World Guide: Destination Canada.
www.lonelyplanet.com/destinations/north_america/canada

Royal Canadian Mounted Police. www.rcmp-grc.gc.ca

Statistics Canada. www.statcan.ca

The Weather Network (Canadian weather information). www.theweathernetwork.com

The World Bank Group (type "Canada" in the search box). www.worldbank.org

VIDEOS

Canada: A Magnificent Journey. 3 volumes. Toronto: Good Earth Productions, 2001. (VHS)

Canada: A People's History. Canadian Broadcasting Corporation, 2000, 2003. (DVD)

BIBLIOGRAPHY

Canada: A Portrait. Ottawa: Statistics Canada, 1992.

Dryden, Ken. *Home Game: Hockey and Life in Canada.* Toronto: McClelland and Stewart, 1989.

Francis, Daniel. *The Imaginary Indian: The Image of the Indian in Canadian Culture.* Vancouver: Arsenal Pulp Press, 1992.

Hacker, Carlotta. *The Book of Canadians: An Illustrated Guide to Who Did What.* Edmonton: Hurtig Publishers, 1983.

Lipset, Seymour M. *Continental Divide: Values and Institutions in Canada and the United States.* New York: Routledge, 1991.

Lunn, Janet, and Christopher Moore. *The Story of Canada.* Toronto: Lester Publishing and Key Porter Books, 1992.

Malcolm, Andrew. *The Canadians.* New York: St. Martin, 1991.

Morris, Jan. *O Canada: Travels in an Unknown Country.* HarperCollins, 1992.

Richardson, Bill. *Canada Customs: Droll Recollections, Musings and Quibbles.* Vancouver: Brighouse Press, 1988.

Watson, Jessie and Wreford Watson: *The Canadians: How they live and work.* Toronto: Griffin Press Ltd., 1977.

Woodcock, George: *The Canadians.* Don Mills: Fitzhenry and Whiteside, 1979.

INDEX